T0407559

Kari Stenman
Karolina Hołda

Finnish
Bomber Colours
1939–1945

STRATUS

Published in Poland in 2018
by STRATUS sp.j.
Po. Box 123,
27-600 Sandomierz 1, Poland
e-mail: office@mmpbooks.biz
for
Mushroom Model
Publications,
e-mail: rogerw@mmpbooks.biz

ISBN
978-83-65281-03-6

Editor in chief
Roger Wallsgrove

Editorial Team
Bartłomiej Belcarz
Robert Pęczkowski
Artur Juszczak

Text and research
Kari Stenman

Colour profiles
Karolina Hołda

Proofreading
Roger Wallsgrove

DTP
Bartłomiej Belcarz

Printed by
Drukarnia Diecezjalna,
ul. Żeromskiego 4,
27-600 Sandomierz
www.wds.pl
marketing@wds.pl

Table of contents

Acknowledgements

Most of the facts presented in this book have been drawn from the Finnish National Archives, from its Sörnäinen division, which was previously the Finnish War Archives. The documents consulted were the order files by the Air Force Headquarters dealing with the national and serial markings as well as camouflage. Another valuable source of information was the individual aircraft files, which held also the repair reports, usually containing also the painting statements.

I am indebted to the staff of this organization, having fulfilled my enquiries by delivering masses of archive files for my use, during the past forty-five years.

Thank you is also due to the staffs of the Finnish Air Force Museum, Finnish Aviation Museum and Finnish War Museum, for a practically free access to their collections, whether material, documents or photos.

The bulk of the photos and especially the high quality ones came from the Finnish Defence Force collections, shortly abbreviated as SA-kuva. Thank you for making them available to the public.

I also wish to extend my gratitude to many bomber pilots, navigators and gunners, who shared their personal log books and photo albums. I would especially like to mention the late *ev.* Raoul Harju-Jeanty, late *ev.* Aimo Huhtala, *late ev.* Martti Uotinen, *late ev.* Risto Pajari, late *ev.luutn.* Armas Eskola, late *ev.luutn.* Tauno Kangas and late *ev.luutn.* Erik Stenbäck.

Photos were also received from the following wartime members of the Finnish Air Force: Lars Bergman, A. Bremer, Carl-Erik Bruun, Oiva Eerola, Oiva Halmetoja, Tuuri Heporauta, Tauno Iisalo, Aimo Juhola, Kaarlo Juurikas, Kyösti Karhila, Olli Kepsu, Lauri Kippo, Ilpo Koskinen, Reino Lampelto, Tapani Lampimäki, Lauri Lehtomäki, Unto Oksala, Martti Perälä, Matti Poutvaara, Osmo Rantala, Olli Riekki, Otto Rautanen, Esko Rinne, Ilpo Ritavuori, Lauri Räätäri, Paavo Saari, Juhani Suomalainen, Kurt Södergård, Aarne Tirkkonen, Jorma Turpeinen, Erkki Uotinen, Kullervo Virtanen, Toivo Vuorinen and Lauri Äijö. Thank you all.

The support of my fellow researchers late Eino Ritaranta, Lassi Eskola, Pentti Manninen, Klaus Niska, Kyösti Partonen and Carl-Fredrik Geust is duly acknowledged. All expressed no limitations to my wishes concerning their collections, photos, drawings or otherwise.

Last but not least I wish to thank Karolina Holda, the illustrator of this book. She has shown exceptional talent in the faithful reproduction of the colour profiles. With a keen eye to the smallest detail, she was also open to all my instructions. The end result being a series of the finest Finnish bomber profiles that have ever appeared in print.

Fokker C.X

As a natural replacement for the ageing Dutch Fokker C.V reconnaissance and light bomber aircraft, the Finnish Air Force opted for Fokker's newer type, the C.X. Four aircraft were bought from Holland on 18 May 1936 and also a licence to manufacture the type at the State Aircraft Factory. The Dutch aircraft were shipped to Finland, arriving on 16 January 1937, with serials for the I series being FK-78 to FK-81.

The order for licence production was placed on 12 October 1936 for 14 aircraft of the II series, increased on 12 February 1937 by 16 aircraft of the III series. The former batch was manufactured between January and June 1938 with serials FR-82 to FK-94 and the latter between June and December 1938 with serials FK-95 to FK-111.

On 24 April 1942 the air force HQ accepted the State Aircraft Factory offer for five additional C.Xs of the IV series, these being completed in December 1942 with serials FK-111 to FK-115, the first one being issued for the second time. The Finnish Air Force had a total of 39 Fokker C.X aircraft.

Winter War

The army co-op squadrons LLv 12 and LLv 14 of LeR 1 flew with the Fokker C.X from 1 December 1939 on reconnaissance missions, where the advance and spearheads of the Soviet armies could be established on both sides of Lake Ladoga. Harassment bombings were carried out whenever possible.

LLv 10 was the only dive-bombing element of LeR 1 and the squadron was subordinated directly to General Headquarters for its use against specified targets. Action had to wait three weeks.

On 18 December a Fokker C.X pair of LLv 14 did not get to the reconnaissance area in the eastern part of the Karelian Isthmus due to enemy fighters. One became the first one to be chased by fighters, luckily at the end of the mission. The pilot, *kers.* Martti Perälä, dodged the attack by a tight turn, and then pulled up into a cloud.

Fokker C.X, serial FK-78, of Lentolaivue 10 (LLv 10) parked at Suur-Merijoki near Viipuri on 28 April 1938. The aircraft has an offensive load of two 100 kg and eight 25 kg bombs. This plane was built in the Netherlands and wore the local Camouflage Bruin (Dark Brown) upper sides with aluminium lacquer lower sides (Finnish Air Force)

On 23 December the weather became clear. LLv 10 dive-bombed a column at Perkjärvi with seven C.X planes, causing one truck to catch fire and broke the column. After this the HQ kept the squadron as a reserve.

LLv 12 flew six bombing sorties to the Vipuri-Leningrad railway, attacking Perkjärvi station. 7 IAP fighters were directed to the target and one Fokker C.X was shot down near Johannes.

On 19 January LLv 10 dive-bombed motorized troops crammed into Pitkäranta industrial area. Seven Fokkers led by *luutn.* Pietarinen caused great confusion amongst the Russians, destroying several trucks and buildings.

At dusk LLv 12 bombed on four occasions in nine sorties a base on the ice of lake Kirkkojärvi holding twelve I-16 fighters. The bombs were seen to have hit eight of them.

On 22 January LLv 10 carried out the following squadron bombing, when seven aircraft dive-bombed an air base on the ice of lake Karkunlampi on the east coast of Lake Ladoga. The inaccurate information of the location of the aircraft rows caused the bombs to miss just by one length of the aircraft, but possibly breaking the ice.

An aviation parade of Lentorykmentti *1 was held at Suur-Merijoki on 16 May 1939. Here are all thirteen Fokker C.Xs of* Lentolaivue *12 in a line-up. The neat and clean planes are, from the camera, FK-102, 105, 93. (Finnish Air Force)*

On 29 January several vessels were observed to arrive at Saunasaari base from Lake Ladoga. Six dive-bombers of LLv 10 attacked a large cargo ship and an icebreaker anchored at Saunasaari quay on the south-western coast. The bombs crossed both vessels, damaging both. The extremely sharp and accurate anti-aircraft fire shot down one C.X and ripped off the landing gear from another. Recent research shows that sweeper No. 32 was sunk and No. 34 severely damaged, both vessels belonging to the Lake Ladoga Naval Detachment.

On 1 February 1940 LLv 12 photographed at noon in bright daylight the front on the Karelian Isthmus. *Ylik.* Marttila and *ylik.* Salminen manned FK-105 and the clear pictures revealed the spearhead of the new Russian offensive. Four Fokker fighters from LLv 24 escorted and 7 IAP fighters shot down one Fokker D.XXI while protecting the photo plane from the attack of about 40 enemy fighters.

During February and in darkness the Fokker C.Xs both reconnoitred and performed harassment bombings. Camp fires had proved to be good target markers and the visibility against the white snowy ground was good.

Ten Fokker dive-bombers of LLv 10 in a line-up at Suur-Merijoki on 16 May 1939. The closest aircraft are FK-109, 108, 89. A few months later in the Winter War LLv 10 was a dedicated dive-bombing unit. (Finnish Air Force)

From 10 October 1939 large war games were arranged in Finland, serving also as the mobilization for the Winter War. During these rehearsals many aircraft received additional camouflage, shown here on FK-80 of LLv 10, as seen in flight on 24 November 1939, just one week before the conflict. (Finnish Air Force)

On 3 March the Russians commenced their advance across the frozen gulf of Viipuri (Vyborg). Next day the Soviet troops managed to cross the Gulf of Viipuri over the ice and formed a bridgehead at Vilaniemi and Häränpääniemi. Troops and columns flowed across the ice from Pulliniemi and Tuppura. All air regiments were thrown in to repel this serious threat.

In seven days the ice over the Gulf of Viipuri was swept clean causing heavy casualties to the Russians. The advance was stopped and Viipuri remained unconquered.

LeR 1 employed LLv 10 and 12 to the Gulf of Viipuri. The reconnaissance of the latter provided a good picture of the spearhead of the Soviet advances. The bombings were more in the nature of harassment, due to the modest bomb load of the Fokker C.X.

On 13 March the Winter war ended at 11.00 hours, under the terms of the peace treaty negotiated in Moscow.

Fokker C.Xs had performed 587 sorties during the war, dropping 66.7 tons of bombs. By squadron the sorties were divided as follows: LLv 10 – 135, LLv 12 – 307 and LLv 14 – 145. Eight aircraft were lost on operations and fifteen airmen were killed or missing in action.

Continuation War

At the mobilization, beginning on 18 June 1941, the army co-op squadrons became independent and were subjected directly to the army groups. LLv 12 and 16 were tasked for the use of the Karelian Army, tasked with the re-occupation of the lost territory north and north-east of Lake Ladoga. LLv 14 was under command of the Karelian Isthmus army.

On 25 June, the opening day of the Continuation war, these three squadrons had 17 serviceable Fokker C.Xs on duty, tasked with reconnaissance, artillery fire-control, tactical photography, leaflet dropping and bombing missions.

On 12 July 3/LLv 12 was tasked with a mission to bomb Jänisjärvi station with three C.Xs led by *kapt.* Magnusson. The attack was carried out at 00.05 hours on the given target, all bombs hit the rail yard, several wagons of the four trains at the station caught fire and the rails were rendered inoperable.

On 21 July a C.X scout of 3/LLv 12 was jumped by enemy fighters north of Lake Ladoga. After the reconnaissance, five I-153s and five I-16s appeared from the south. The C.X broke off into a vertical dive, at the beginning of which one I-16 followed, but not down to the surface. Small bombs were observed under the wings of the I-153s.

FK-88 of LLv 14 basking in the sun on the hardstand at Utti on 14 July 1940. The squadron was one of three flying the C.X, though only partially equipped with the type in the Winter War a few months earlier. (Finnish Air Force)

FK-103 of 3/LLv 12 preparing for a mission from Mikkeli on 27 June 1941. Below the second man from the left, wearing a parachute, is the flight leader kapt. *Ragnar Magnusson. The plane is a typical example of hastily applied yellow eastern front markings in the unit, on the fuselage over the serial number. (SA-kuva)*

On 4 September in the attack preparations of the Karelian Army, 3/LLv 12 controlled artillery fire south of Tuulos with one plane. An enemy artillery position with 7–8 guns was shelled. It was observed that the shells exploded in the middle of the firing position. An ammunition storage or pile blew up.

The autumn was spent in continuous reconnaissance for the advancing Finnish troops and harassment bombardments of Soviet land forces and equipment.

On 26 October 3/LLv 14 handed over its C.Xs to LLv 16. By this time LLv 14 had lost three C.Xs in combat and one in a flying accident, killing eight airmen.

On 7 November one C.X plane of 3/LLv 12 was harassed by a MiG-3 fighter. The pilot *kopr.* Suvanto handled the situation well, when all of a sudden one enemy attacked from above and behind. Suvanto went in a dive and during it made an aileron turn to the opposite direction. The enemy fighter made three passes from ahead, five from the rear and side and five from above and behind, during about 10 minutes. The observer fired several machine-gun bursts towards the

attacking plane, which had to dodge. Above them flew 18 MiG-3s heading to the west. By flying right down to the surface, the pilot managed to break off from the enemy, which finally pulled up and joined the formation flying above. In an inspection made after the flight four holes in the wings were observed.

The attrition during the Finnish advance was very high and at the beginning 1942 LLv 12 and LLv 16 had in total just one C.X plane airworthy.

On 19 April 3/LLv 16 made a typical bombing sortie to Murmansk railway with one C.X piloted by *ltm.* Rantala with *luutn.* Kahla as observer. At 21.05 three km north of Urosozero station they observed a southbound train with 35 wagons, bombed it from 500 metres with 2x100 kg and 8x12.5 kg bombs. Small bombs partly hit the train, the big bombs hit the rail bank alongside the train and in front of it. Half an hour later the train stood about 300 m from the previous location, burned and exploded. The train was then strafed.

On 26 April 1942 the first Mannerheim Cross to a reconnaissance airman was awarded to *luutn.* Paavo Kahla. He had earlier flown with 3/LLv 14 and was presently an observer with 3/LLv 16 and had flown 150 missions.

FK-97 of 3/LLv 16 ready for a mission from Viiksjärvi, near Karhumäki, in March 1942. The regular pilot was ltm. Osmo Rantala, a future Ju 88 dive-bomber pilot. The Warpaint is quite fresh, being applied on 24 January 1942, with Light Grey undersides. (Osmo Rantala)

On 3 May, while the fronts had remained calm for six months and the Finns were waiting for the outcome of the world war, a re-organization was made in the air arm based on territorial division.

On the Olonets Isthmus *Lentorykmentti* 1 was re-formed to operate for the Olonets Group. LeR 1 was seconded two squadrons: LeLv 12 already reconnoitering in the sector and LeLv 32 for fighter duties. The operational area was specified as the Olonets isthmus and the nearby waterways.

Lentorykmentti 2 continued to operate for the Maaselkä Group. In addition to LeLv 24 and 28 it now included also LeLv 16. In the new sector of LeR 2 was the whole Maaselkä Isthmus and the east coat of Lake Onega.

On 9 May, when aerial reconnaissance discovered that several barges had passed the winter at the mouths of the rivers Vodla and Andoma running into Lake Onega, the task to destroy these was given to LeR 4 and LeR 2, in addition to the saw mill on the river Vodla.

The target for LeR 2 became the barges at the mouth of river Vodla and it commenced the operation five minutes before the Blenheim bombers of LeR 4. Four C.X planes of 3/LeLv 16 bombed the village, setting a house in fire and the barges at the mouth of the river. Right after this six

FK-109 of 3/LLv 16 parked between Karelian houses at Viiksjärvi village on 25 March 1942. The houses provided good shelter for the aircraft and also handy accommodation for the aircrews. The Warpaint of FK-109 was applied on 20 February 1942. (SA-kuva)

FK-99 parked at Utti on 26 May 1942, next to Fokker D.XXIs of T-LeLv 35. FK-99 has just been through a factory repair and is on the way to its unit, 3/LeLv 12 based at Nurmoila in Olonets. (Olli Riekki)

Gladiators of 1/LeLv 16 strafed the target area. LeLv 16 based at Äänislinna repeated the attack with the same units being then the last over the target.

On 18 July a C.X of 3/LeLv 12 was on an artillery fire control mission in the Oresenskyo Lake area, where the Finnish artillery scored several hits in the target. One hit in an ammunition storage and a big explosion was observed.

On 28 July an aerial victory was credited to 3/LeLv 16 leader *kapt.* Lasse Saxell piloting C.X coded FK-78, claiming one Polikarpov R-5 biplane shot down in the twilight over Maaselkä isthmus.

FK-109 of 3/LeLv 16 flipped on landing at Hirvas on 12 August 1942. The aircraft was hit by flak and the observer, luutn. *Paavo Kahla, climbed outside onto the dead pilot's lap and flew back to base, but could not pull the stick back enough on landing. (Esko Rinne)*

FK-110 of 3/LeLv 12 landed too steeply at Nurmoila on the night of 30 August 1942 and bellied in. It is seen here moved near a service hangar and about to be sent by rail to the factory for repairs. The Warpaint is fresh, being applied on 20 June 1942. (Finnish Air Force)

On 21 August 3/LeLv 16 was tasked to attack gun boats on southern Lake Onega. Eight Moranes of LeLv 28 took off to fly escort. They bombed a gunboat at Muroskoyeo Lake with 4x100 kg and 15x12.5 kg bombs, hitting the deck with at least four small bombs.

At the beginning of 1943 there were six airworthy Fokker C.Xs serving with 3/LeLv 12, 3/LeLv 16 and 3/LeLv 26. There was very little activity on the ground.

On 19 May the 2nd and 3rd Flights of LeLv 16 flew a joint operation by bombing a fuel storage nearby Juka station. Just before midnight five Fokker C.Xs and three Lysanders dropped from 900 metres a total of 13x100 kg mine bombs, 35x15 kg incendiaries and 32x12.5 kg splinter bombs. Two explosions occurred in the storage area creating high and strong flames. Juka station received 8x15 kg incendiaries lighting one fire.

On 22 June LeLv 16 flew another squadron bombing by attacking an ammunition storage depot north-east of Haapaselkä. At 21.40 hours four C.Xs and three Lysanders dropped from 900 metres 10x100 kg mine bombs and 67x15 kg incendiaries, hitting in the target area, where one strong explosion was observed.

FK-104 of 3/LeLv 12 parked at Nurmoila shortly before it was damaged by a Russian fighter on 20 July 1942, and sent to the factory for repairs. The Warpaint was applied on 27 April 1942 with Light Grey undersides. (Kari Stenman coll.)

FK-110 of 3/LeLv 12 photographed from the roof of Nurmoila servicing hangar in August 1942, showing clearly the pattern of Warpaint on the Fokker C.X. Apart from the national markings and serials, no other marking have been recorded on the C.X. (Finnish Air Force)

On 27 July LeLv 16 performed the last joint bombing mission by attacking a base at the Voivanets river in the Maaselkä Isthmus. At 21.40 four C.Xs and two Lysanders dropped 10x100 kg mine bombs and 55x15 kg incendiaries from 900 metres. Two small fires were lit. The damage inflicted with these joint attacks was not considered worthwhile.

From this onwards the missions were flown by single aircraft, tasks including mostly reconnaissance, leaflet dropping and tactical photography, over very quiet front lines.

When 1944 started there were still eight Fokker C.Xs flying with 3/LeLv 12, 3/LeLv 16 and 3/LeLv 26.

TLeLv 12 flew its last mission with the C.X on 2 June 1944, HLeLv 26 followed suit a fortnight later and TLeLv 16 flew it last C.X mission on 31 August 1944, just five days before the Continuation War ended in a cease-fire.

TLeLv 12 had lost five C.Xs, four in combat, with three airmen killed and one captured. TLeLv 16 had lost eleven C.Xs, of which four were in combat, with nine airmen killed. HLeLv 26 lost one C.X in a flying accident with no personnel casualties.

During the autumn of 1944 two C.Xs were still deployed against the Germans in Lapland, where one plane with crew was lost to flak. The C.X continued to fly after the war mostly in target-towing and communications duties until January 1958, when the last one crashed.

S/n	C/n	Delivered	Struck off charge	Remarks	Flying Hours
FK-78	5828	11 Jun 1937	1 Feb 1943	W/o Lake Onega 9 Dec 1942	659.45
FK-79	5829	3 Nov 1937	9 Aug 1944	W/o Hirvas 9 Apr 1944	631.30
FK-80	5830	12 Nov 1937	20 Sep 1941	W/o Käkisalmi 16 Aug 1941	343.40
FK-81	5831	2 Apr 1938	11 Mar 1940	W/o Uuksu 26 Jan 1940	232.25
FK-82	II/1	11 Jan 1938	2 Nov 1940	W/o Siilinjärvi 26 Jun 1940	132.50
FK-83	II/2	13 Feb 1938	22 Feb 1941	W/o Rissala 27 Jan 1941	283.40
FK-84	II/3	8 Apr 1938	30 Jan 1941	W/o Taipalsaari 30 Aug 1940	517.25
FK-85	II/4	11 Apr 1938	5 Oct 1943	W/o Immola 19 Aug 1943	686.50
FK-86	II/5	5 May 1938	19 Sep 1942	W/o Hirvas 20 Aug 1942	458.25
FK-87	II/6	13 May 1938	11 Mar 1940	W/o Pitkäranta 15 Jan 1940	165.10
FK-88	II/7	21 May 1938	20 May 1942	W/o Äänislinna 30 Oct 1941	378.15
FK-89	II/8	19 May 1938	6 Nov 1941	W/o Tienhaara 24 Sep 1941	263.05
FK-90	II/9	21 May 1938	30 Aug 1941	W/o Ilmee 31 Jul 1941	207
FK-91	II/10	8 Jun 1938	17 Dec 1941	W/o Tohmajärvi 13 Jul 1941	206.10
FK-92	II/11	14 Jun 1938	20 May 1942	W/o Ääninen 10 Dec 1941	412.50
FK-93	II/12	16 Jun 1938	30 Dec 1939	W/o Kivennapa 1 Dec 1939	123.55
FK-94	II/13	16 Jun 1938	9 Aug 1944	W/o Hirvas 9 Apr 1944	300+
FK-95	II/14	19 Dec 1938	11 Mar 1940	W/o Johannes 19 Dec 1939	113.45
FK-96	III/1	20 Jun 1938	25 May 1940	W/o Uusikirkko 23 Dec 1939	173.35
FK-97	III/2	22 Jun 1938	13 Nov 1942	W/o Kontupohja 28 Aug 1942	366.30
FK-98	III/3	22 Jun 2938	1 Oct 1952	Last flight 17 Nov 1944	695.05
FK-99	III/7	28 Jun 1938	16 Jan 1946	W/o Pirkkala 11 Dec 1945	609.50
FK-100	III/4	4 Jul 1938	15 Aug 1941	W/o Papero 21 Jul 1941	392.40
FK-101	III/5	12 Jul 1938	30 Dec 1939	W/o Heinjoki 4 Dec 1939	153.15
FK-102	III/6	11 Jul 1938	13 Dec 1939	W/o Simpele 2 Dec 1939	171.45

The observer carries a hand camera to FK-109 of 3/LLv 16, about to take off for a flight from Viiksjärvi on 25 March 1942. The mission turned out to be a 15 minute machine-gun testing, piloted by the flight leader kapt. Lasse Saxell. *(SA-kuva)*

FK-103	III/8	14 Jul 1938	2 Feb 1943	W/o Nurmoila 21 Jan 1943	300.45
FK-104	III/9	15 Jul 1938	8 Dec 1944	W/o Kittilä 23 Oct 1944	633.35
FK-105	III/10	20 Jul 1938	13 Sep 1941	W/o Läskelä 5 Aug 1941	244.50
FK-106	III/11	19 Jul 1938	6 Nov 1941	W/o Pyhäjärvi 11 Sep 1941	225.25
FK-107	III/13	23 Jul 1938	30 Jan 1942	W/o Lotinanpelto 23 Nov 1941	362.15
FK-108	III/14	26 Jul 1938	30 Aug 1941	W/o Kirvu 31 Jul 1941	249.40
FK-109	III/12	22 Jul 1938	1 Mar 1945	W/o Säämäjärvi 17 Aug 1944	523.30
FK-110	III/15	28 Jul 1938	1 Oct 1952	W/o Onttola 8 Aug 1944	366.35
FK-111	III/16	29 Jul 1938	11 Mar 1940	W/o Saunasaari 29 Jan 1940	94
FK-111	IV/1	1 Jan 1943	30 Jun 1958	W/o Koivulahti 25 Jan 1958	1635.25
FK-112	IV/2	15 Dec 1942	25 Aug 1943	W/o Sumeri 8 Jun 1943	74.30
FK-113	IV/3	28 Dec 1942	1 Oct 1952	W/o Urjala 26 Apr 1950	990.20
FK-114	IV/4	31 Dec 1942	6 Oct 1958	Last flight 8 Feb 1955	829.05
FK-115	IV/5	9 Jan 1943	1 Oct 1952	W/o Tuusula 22 Dec 1950	667.35

Fokker C.X
Camouflage and markings

The four Dutch-built aircraft (FK-78–81) were painted in local colours with *Camouflage Bruin* upper sides and aluminium lacquer lower sides. Two of these (FK-78 and 79) were re-painted before the Winter War with Finnish Olive Green upper sides with Light Grey lower sides.

The first two batches of licence produced aircraft (FK-82–111) in 1938 received the contemporary standard camouflage of Olive Green upper sides and Light Grey lower sides.

After the introduction of the Black and Olive Green Warpaint on 30 September 1940, the first C.X to get this camouflage was FK-100 on 18 January 1941, followed by FK-106 in June and FK-98 in September 1941.

Fokker C.X serial FK-81 at the State Aircraft Factory at Tampere in December 1937. The aircraft is Dutch-built with Camouflage Bruin (Dark Brown) top sides and aluminium dope undersides. The Fokker logo on the fin existed only on these planes. (State Aircraft Factory)

During the first half of 1942 ten more C.Xs received the Warpaint, in chronological order FK-94, 97, 109, 85, 103, 104, 99, 86, 79 and 110.

The *DN-väri** underside colour was introduced on 7 May 1942 and this was applied first to FK-104 on 15 January 1943, followed by FK-94, 110, 109 and 98 during 1943 and FK-79 and 99 the next year.

The last licence produced batch (FK-111–115), which was manufactured during the latter half of 1942, received Warpaint with *DN-väri* undersides at the factory.

These colours remained on the C.Xs to the end of the 1940s, the Black and Olive Green Warpaint being officially abandoned in September 1947.

FK-97 of LLv 12 seen at Suur-Merijoki on 18 January 1939. The aircraft came from the factory production line six months earlier with contemporary single colour Olive Green upper surfaces and Light Grey lower surfaces. (Finnish Air Force)

*   See page 218.

FK-80 of 3/LLv 14 hidden between the trees at the edge of Lappeenranta airfield on 14 August 1941. This plane was painted in Finnish colours in a factory repair in September 1940, just before the introduction of the Warpaint. (SA-kuva)

FK-103 of 3/LeLv 12 taxied into a filled bomb crater at Nurmoila on 24 May 1942 and ended on its nose. The standard wing camouflage pattern is clearly seen here. The Warpaint is only a month old. (Finnish Air Force)

The engine of 3/LeLv 12's FK-111 cut on take off from Nurmoila on 21 February 1943. In a forced landing on a frozen lake the landing gear was smashed off by a jetty. The aircraft has two month old Warpaint with DN-väri undersides. (SA-kuva)

FK-98 of LeLv 26 parked at Kilpasilta in the summer of 1943. The Warpaint, with DN-väri undersides, was factory applied on 5 May 1943. The yellow eastern front markings under both wing tips are standard. (Olli Riekki)

Fokker CX, FK-80, luutn. Heikki Kalaja, leader of 1/Lento-laivue 10, Mensuvaara airfield, January 1940. Camouflage colours: upper surfaces Camouflage Bruin (Dark Brown), under surfaces aluminium dope. Serial Black, Fokker logo White.

FK-80 of LLv 10 tucked into a servicing tent, which was erected in the hangar at Suur-Merijoki, as photographed on 30 March 1938. This Dutch-built machine has Dark Brown upper surfaces, with the Fokker logo on the fin. (Finnish Air Force)

Fokker CX, FK-85, kers. Pentti Rekola, 2/Lentolaivue 10, Lappeenranta airfield, February 1940. Camouflage colours: upper surfaces Olive Green, under surfaces Light Grey. Serial Black.

FK-85 of LLv 10 in flight over Viipuri on 11 May 1939. The paintwork is the contemporary factory camouflage of Olive Green tops and Light Grey bottoms. As can be seen here the colours are rather glossy. (Finnish Air Force)

Fokker CX, FK-110, vääp. Martti Perälä, 3/Lentolaivue 14, Lappeenranta airfield, September 1941. Camouflage colours: upper surfaces Olive Green, under surfaces Light Grey. Standard Eastern Front markings Yellow, serial Black.

FK-110 of 3/LLv 14 at Lappeenranta in September 1941. Noteworthy is the yellow nose ring, which was not applied to all C.Xs. The camouflage colour is still the factory applied Olive Green from 1938. (Toivo Vuorinen)

Fokker CX, FK-86, kers. Erkki Karhu, 3/Lentolaivue 12, Mantsi landing ground, September 1941. Camouflage colours: upper surfaces Olive Green, under surfaces Light Grey. Standard Eastern Front markings Yellow, serial Black.

FK-86 of 3/LeLv 12 made a hard landing at Mantsi island on 11 September 1941, slicing off the landing gear. This plane was also one of few to wear the Yellow nose ring, which was added to single-engine warplanes on 1 September. (SA-kuva)

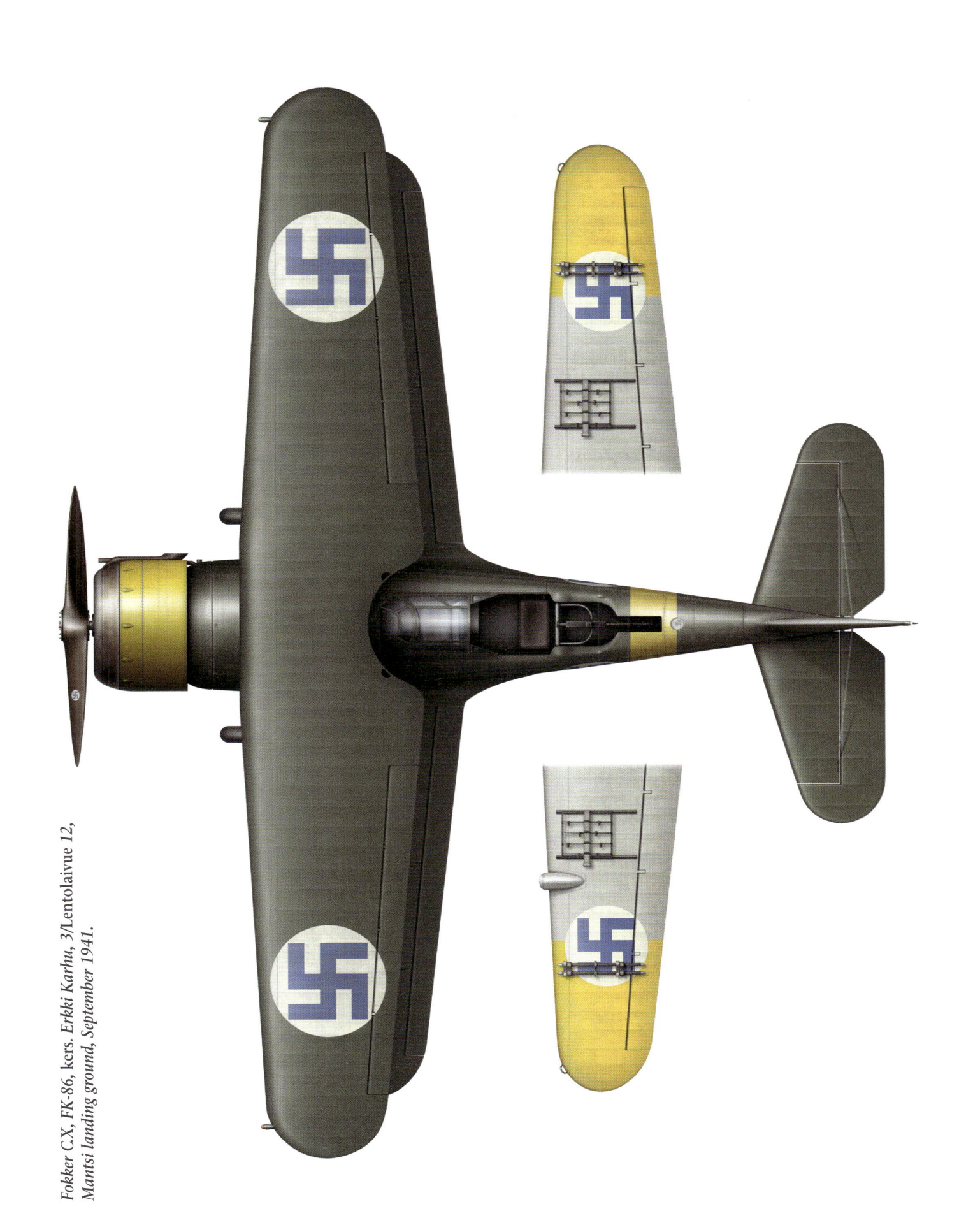

Fokker C.X, FK-86, kers. Erkki Karhu, 3/Lentolaivue 12, Mantsi landing ground, September 1941.

23

Fokker CX, FK-106, alikers. Eino Suvanto, 3/Lentolaivue 12, Mikkeli airfield, June 1941. Camouflage colours: upper surfaces Olive Green and Black, under surfaces Light Grey. Standard Eastern Front markings Yellow, serial Black and Olive Green.

FK-106 of 3/LLv 12 about to take off on a mission from Mikkeli on 27 June 1941, when this plane performed five photographic sorties over the border. The Warpaint and yellow eastern front identifications markings were hastily applied at the factory on 20 June 1941. (SA-kuva)

Fokker C.X, FK-109, kers. Orvo Sarin, 3/Lentolaivue 16, Viiksjärvi landing ground, March 1942. Camouflage colours: upper surfaces Olive Green and Black, under surfaces Light Grey. Standard Eastern Front markings Yellow, serial Black, skis aluminium dope.

FK-109 of 3/LLv 16 returned to Viiksjärvi forward base from a short flight on 26 March 1942. The aircraft was pushed into a shelter between the Karelian log houses. The Warpaint is fresh, as it was applied at the factory on 20 February 1942. This plane was damaged on 12 August 1942 in a landing accident, ending its career with this unit. (SA-kuva)

Fokker C.X, FK-99, maj. Auvo Maunula, commander of Lentolaivue 12, Nurmoila airfield, July 1942. Camouflage colours: upper surfaces Olive Green and Black, under surfaces Light Grey. Standard Eastern Front markings Yellow, number Black.

(Pages 26 and 27) FK-99 of 3/LeLv 12 captured by an official photographer at Nurmoila on 2 August 1942. It has standard period Warpaint applied at the factory on 16 May 1942, but still with Light Grey undersides, missing the DN-väri only by days. The aircraft served in this unit for almost 16 months, until a landing accident on 14 September 1943. (Finnish Air Force)

Fokker CX, FK-99, maj. Auvo Maunula, commander of Lentolaivue 12, Nurmoila airfield, July 1942.

Fokker CX, FK-99, maj. Auvo Maunula, commander of Lentolaivue 12, Nurmoila airfield, July 1942.

Fokker CX, FK-110, luutn. Pentti Tarkkonen, 3/Lentolaivue 12, Nurmoila airfield, June 1943. Camouflage colours: upper surfaces Olive Green and Black, under surfaces DN-väri. Standard Eastern Front markings Yellow, serial Black.

FK-110 in transit from a factory repair and seen here at Utti. On 4 May 1943 kapt. Erkki Jauri flew the plane to its unit, 3/LeLv 12 based at Nurmoila. The new Warpaint with DN-väri lower surfaces was applied on 9 March 1943. (Finnish Air Force Museum)

Bristol Blenheim I, II & IV

Purchase

The Finnish Ministry of Defence was the first export customer for the Blenheim, placing an order at Bristol on 6 October 1936 for 18 Blenheim Is. These British-built bombers received the Finnish serial numbers BL-104 to BL-121 inclusive. The first two planes arrived in Helsinki on 29 July 1937, the last two being delivered on 27 July 1938. This batch was called series (sarja) I in Finland. They had open bomb bays like inverted chutes.

On 12 April 1938 a production license was acquired, and 15 Blenheim IIs (as the Finnish licence production was officially defined) were subsequently ordered on 6 April 1939 from the State Aircraft Factory (*Valtion lentokonetehdas* – VL). Before series II production started, World War II and the Finnish-Soviet Winter War broke out. Two more batches were ordered from England, which had released the type for delivery to Finland.

Twelve "long-nose" British-built Blenheim IVs (BL-122 to BL-133; series III) were handed over to Finnish crews on 17 January 1940. Ten aircraft arrived in Finland four days later, one aircraft disappeared over the North Sea and the other arrived in Finland on 5 June 1940, after repairs from a landing accident in Sweden.

Series IV consisted of 12 British-built Blenheim Is (BL-134 to BL-145) which arrived in Finland on 26 February 1940, flown in by British volunteer transfer crews.

During the short peace period the aircraft factory started production of the previously ordered series II (BL-146 to BL-160), the first plane being delivered on 14 June 1941 and the last on 9 January 1942. Only these 15 aircraft had bulged bomb bay doors.

On 7 January 1942 an order was placed at the factory for 30 Blenheim IIs (series V, coded BL-161 to BL-190), delivered from 28 July to 26 November 1943 and for 10 Blenheim IVs (series VI, coded BL-196 to BL-205), delivered from 26 February to 15 April 1944. These bombers had as a standard feature the VL-designed carburettor dust filters.

VL State thus produced a total of 45 Blenheim IIs and 10 Blenheim IVs. A further order for five Blenheim IVs, which had been placed on 27 July 1943, was cancelled after the armistice on 19 September 1944. The Finnish Air Force had a total of 97 Blenheims.

Blenheim I, serial BL-105 of Lentolaivue 44, *seen at Immola on 15 November 1937. This machine was one of the first to arrive in Finland, less than three months earlier. It was painted at the Bristol factory in the contemporary Finnish camouflage of Olive Green topsides and aluminium lacquer undersides of flying surfaces. The serial font was British. (Finnish Air Force)*

Winter War

At the beginning of the Winter War the Finnish bombers were concentrated in *Lentorykmentti* 4 with two squadrons, LLv 44 having eight Blenheims and LLv 46 with nine Blenheims. The regiment, commanded by *ev.luutn*. Toivo Somerto, was tasked with bombardment and reconnaissance specified by the supreme command. At the beginning the regiment concentrated on areas lacking other aerial reconnaissance, i.e. north-east of Lake Ladoga and northwards along the border to Uhtua.

From 20 December LeR 4 sorties had to be flown more often at dusk or dawn and at a higher altitude due to the fighter threat. One Blenheim of LLv 46 was chased by three I-16s over Salmi, when the rear gunner managed to shoot down one attacker, the first kill scored by the gunners.

On the morning of 20 January *maj*. Erik Stenbäck of LLv 44 attacked the Karkunlampi base with four Blenheims. They scored several hits among the parked aircraft, just in time before enemy fighters appeared on the scene. On 21 January 10 long-nose Blenheims arrived at Luonetjärvi as new equipment for LLv 46, which took up an extensive training programme for a month.

The bombing of Lotinanpelto air base was delayed by the weather until 26 February. LLv 46 was declared operational and at 3 am took off with eight bombers led by *kapt*. Kepsu to attack Lotinanpelto. Due to poor visibility en route over Lake Ladoga, the aircraft were separated and three aircraft bombed the actual target, one aircraft bombed the warehouses at Lotinanpelto station, one bombed the railway at Lotinanpelto, two bombed the village of Vitele and one bombed the artillery battery at Yhinmäki. As a result several fires were observed both at Lotinanpelto and Vitele. In the afternoon another three Blenheims again bombed Lotinanpelto and found eight aircraft destroyed and the hangar on fire.

On 16 January 1940 LLv 42 was established and *kapt*. Armas Eskola was put in command. Ten days later English crews flew 12 Blenheims to Juva base as new equipment.

From 27 February all LeR 4 sorties were flown over the Karelian Isthmus. The second attack by the Russians had broken the outer defence lines and their troops approached Viipuri (Vyborg). Over five days the Blenheims bombed troops, vehicles, rail yards and equipment south and south-east of Viipuri in 33 sorties.

Blenheim IV with serial BL-130 of 1/LLv 46 on a visit to Kauhava on 28 January 1940. This machine was from a twelve aircraft batch brought to Finland by Finnish crews eight days earlier. It is wearing Bristol applied Finnish camouflage similar to Blenheim Is. (Finnish Air Force)

British crews brought twelve Blenheim Is to Juva on 26 February 1940, the recipient was LLv 42. Above and centre is BL-134, which had civil code OH-IPA during the transfer flight. At bottom OH-IPD taxies at Juva on 26 February 1940. This plane became BL-137 of 3/LLv 42. (Finnish Air Force)

On 4 March Soviet troops had managed to cross the Gulf of Viipuri over the ice and formed a bridgehead at Vilaniemi and Häränpääniemi. Troops and columns flowed across the ice. LeR 4 was ordered to attack with all available forces against the enemy, which was intruding to the west coast of the Gulf of Viipuri. Both LLv 44 and 42, for which this was the baptism of fire, flew strike sorties with five aircraft to the outer Gulf of Finland, where enemy troops were marching towards the Finnish coast.

By 11 March the ice over the Gulf of Viipuri was swept clean, causing heavy casualties to the Russians. The advance on the continent had also been stopped and Viipuri remained unconquered. The Blenheims of LeR 4 had flown 144 sorties over the Gulf of Viipuri.

On 13 March the Winter War ended at 11.00 hours in the peace negotiated in Moscow. *Lentorykmentti* 4 squadrons had carried out 423 sorties, by squadron: LLv 44 – 209, LLv 46 – 152 and LLv 46 – 62 sorties. 131 tons of bombs had been dropped. Seven Blenheims and thirteen crew members were lost in action. The rear gunners shot down five fighters.

BL-105 of LLv 44 on a visit to Petsamo between the wars in August 1940. Behind is a Dragon Rapide of Aero Oy, the Finnish airlines. The Blenheim has been repaired from Winter War combat damage and applied with regulation Finnish font serials. (Kari Stenman coll.)

Blenheim line-up of Lentolaivue 42 at Luonetjärvi in August 1940. Closest are BL-145 and 141. This batch of twelve Blenheim I bombers had standard British late 1930's bomber camouflage of Dark Green and Dark Earth over Black. (Finnish Air Force)

Continuation War

On 25 June 1941 the bomber command LeR 4 had three squadrons. LLv 42 possessed nine Blenheims, LLv 44 eight and LLv 46 three.

The main operational direction of the regiment was specified as the Karelian Isthmus. LLv 42 and LLv 44 received offensive tasks, which were aimed to hamper troop and material transports, harass these connections and raid air bases. LLv 46 was tasked with the long-range reconnaissance needed by the supreme command, but became inactive after two weeks.

On 1 July the first squadron bombardment was carried out by LLv 44, which bombed at dawn the railway between Suojärvi and Säämäjärvi with seven aircraft led by *maj.* Erik Stenbäck. The rails were cut in several places and one train destroyed.

On 8 July *maj.* Eskola of LLv 42 bombed Elisenvaara station at 9 pm, first with eight aircraft and two hours later with nine aircraft. Good hits were scored all over the railyard, trains and wagons.

On 11 July LLv 42 bombed at dawn the station at Antrea with nine aircraft led by *maj.* Eskola. A train was moving in the station but most of the bombs overshot. A few fires in the buildings were observed, including the engine garage.

On 14 July LLv 42 bombed Suojärvi station at 18.10 hours with eight aircraft led by *luutn.* Niilo Hakala, where three trains were with 30–50 wagons and another 40 wagons on a rail extension. High columns of smoke were observed in the target.

The first aircraft of the II series, BL-146, was completed on 14 June 1941, seen here at the roll-out. One month later it was delivered to 2/LLv 44. According to Bristol records this was a Blenheim II. (State Aircraft Factory)

On 19 July LLv 44 bombed at 05.35, with *maj*. Erik Stenbäck's eight aircraft, Sakkola airfield on the Karelian Isthmus, where 14–15 aircraft were observed. The bombs were dropped from 200–400 metres, hitting the field and the vicinity of the aircraft parked at the edge of the forest causing a number of fires. Four Brewsters escorted the Blenheims.

At 22.40–22.45 hours six Blenheims of 1/LLv 44 led by *kapt*. Ahmo bombed the airfield at Käkisalmi from 200–300 metres. The hangar and also a fighter in the middle of the field caught fire. On the east side of the field a large fire built up and on the north side a huge explosion was observed.

Next day the CO of LLv 44 *maj*. Stenbäck headed two swarms of four Blenheims with Römpötti airfield as target. From the impact of the first incendiaries an 800 metres high column column of burst up.

By 25 July the strength of LLv 42 was down to four Blenheims and the squadron bombardments were over for now. Their tasks became reconnaissance, photography and harassment bombings between Lake Ladoga and Rukajärvi.

On 3 August *kapt*. Ahmo of 1/LLv 44 bombed with three 3-plane flights troops, vehicles and tanks in the vicinity of Lahdenpohja and repeated the attack after re-fuelling and re-arming. Hits were observed on the road and its close proximity. A Brewster swarm flew escort.

Blenheim I BL-142 of 3/LLv 42 at Luonetjärvi in early July 1941. In front is the gunner alik. *Sulo Rikkinen. The bomber is still in British camouflage, only the yellow fuselage band and lower wing tips have been added. (Armas Eskola)*

Blenheims of Lentolaivue *42 at the dry beach near Joensuu in mid July 1941. The bombers have been camouflaged with nets and tarpaulins. The dark upper surface colours were hardly ideal on the light sand. At bottom the closest plane is BL-139. (SA-kuva)*

BL-143 of 3/LLv 42 on the beach at Joensuu in August 1941. Warpaint was applied during the previous April at the air depot. The wing leading edge shows some significant overspray. (Carl-Erik Bruun)

A German Gefreiter shakes hands with the pilot of BL-143, ylik. Oiva Eerola at Värtsilä on 14 September 1941. The fin still shows the emblem of 108 Sqn, RAF, a previous user of this plane. (SA-kuva)

BL-137 of 1/LLv 42 takes off from Onttola near Joensuu on 21 August 1941, with luutn. Niilo Hakala at the controls. The aircraft wears its second Warpaint, applied after a combat damage repair just a week earlier. (SA-kuva).

BL-116 of 3/LLv 44 takes off from Mikkeli on 31 July 1941 to reconnoitre the area round the river Tuulosjoki, piloted by ltm. Väinö Helanto. The Warpaint is quite recent, being applied at the factory during an accident repair on 20 June 1941. (SA-kuva)

Blenheims of Detachment Havola about to take off from Värtsilä to bomb Suoju station near Petrozavodsk, on 28 September 1941. Closest is BL-111 of 3/LLv 44, piloted by luutn. Jouko Saarinen and the next is BL-138, flown by kers. Erkki Kontiokangas. (Armas Eskola)

On 19 August *kapt.* Halonen bombed, first with seven and then with six Blenheims of LLv 44, retreating vessels outside Puutsalo on Lake Ladoga, and loading places there. Hits on the vessels and on the shore, where troops were loading, were observed.

On 5 September the task of LLv 42 was specified as reconnaissance and harassment bombings of the Murmansk railway and daily reconnoitring of the shipping in Lake Onega. LLv 44 was tasked with the reconnaissance and harassment bombings of traffic south of River Svir and the reconnoitring of the shipping in southern Lake Ladoga.

On 27 September the reinforced LLv 42 twice bombed Suoju rail yard, with a Morane flight escorting on both occasions. The first five-plane detachment reached the target mostly by instrument flying and came out of the cloud just above the target. A total of 28x100 kg and 8x12,5 kg were dropped on the rail yard, hitting moving trains and causing great havoc and some fires.

Next day the Petrozavodsk-Kondupoga railway was bombed at 10 am in several locations by seven Blenheims of LLv 44 and three of LLv 42. Six Brewsters flew escort, effectively keeping the attacking enemy fighters off the bombers. In the afternoon nine Blenheims attacked the same part of the railway. This time the escort was provided by six Brewsters and six Moranes. This was until now the largest Finnish aircraft formation in the sky.

Missions turned into harassment bombardments of the Murmansk railway and on 12 October the line of the aerial guerilla warfare for LLv 42 and LLv 44 was set at Segesha level, the latter working on the north side.

Blenheim attrition was high during the Finnish advance and at the beginning of 1942 the bomber force was rather weak. LLv 42 had only two and LLv 44 five Blenheims, though the war was in a stalemate, which eased the situation.

On 19 March 1942 the Finns decided to take back Suursaari (Gogland) in the middle of the Gulf of Finland when the advance could be made on the ice. LeR 4 flew in support.

On 27 March LeR 4 received an order to bomb the installation on the north end of the island with their whole strength, in two waves. At 04.40 eleven Blenheims headed towards Suursaari in three flights. Only three bombers found the target in poor weather, two became disoriented and crashed. The second wave had to be cancelled.

On 2 April *ev.luutn.* Olavi Sarko was appointed as the new commander of *Lentorykmentti* 4. Due to the strong Russian flak and fighter threat it was decided to fly the mission under the cover of the darkness: take-off at night, bombing at dawn and return in daylight. Also the full power of the whole regiment was exploited in concentrated strikes.

Blenheim IV serial BL-129 of 1/LLv 44 at Onttola in February 1942. The flight leader, kapt. Esko Ahtiainen, was assigned to this plane. The lower surfaces are still in the regulation aluminium lacquer, but on 19 March 1942 Ahtiainen gave an order to paint them in Light Blue-Grey (RLM 65). (Finnish Air Force)

BL-154 of 2/LLv 42 at Värtsilä in March 1942. This aircraft exploded above the target on 15 April 1942, when bombing the supply area of Varbinitsy. It was probably hit by flak in the darkness. (Finnish Air Force)

BL-160 of 2/LLv 42 at Värtsilä in March 1942. The Finnish-built batches (II and V series) were Blenheim IIs. The best identification for the 15 bombers (BL-146–160) of the II series of was the bulged bomb bay doors. (Kari Stenman coll.)

On 5 April LeR 4 carried out the first joint operation of all three squadrons. The target was the most important Soviet air base in Karelia, Segesha, which was extended in winter to the ice on nearby lake Akanjärvi. Twenty-one aircraft took off for the mission. At dawn seven Blenheims of LLv 42 and another four of LLv 44 bombed Segesha, hitting the rows of planes and barracks.

On 15 April LeR 4 participated in repelling a Soviet infantry offensive on the central River Svir by bombing the warehouse and camp areas. The whole regiment made a nocturnal attack against the Varbinitsy supply centre. LLv 44 participated with three Blenheims and LLv 42 with seven Blenheims, losing three to the intense flak.

BL-115 of 1/LeLv 44 at Onttola after arriving at the unit on 4 June 1942. The flight leader, kapt. Erkki Itävuori, regularly flew this bomber. The machine wears its second Warpaint with aluminium lacquer undersides, which was applied at the factory on 27 May 1942. (Finnish Air Force)

On 9 May, when the aerial reconnaissance had discovered that several barges had passed the winter at the mouths of rivers Vodla and Andoma, running into Lake Onega, the task to destroy these was given to LeR 4 and LeR 2, in addition to the saw mill at river Vodla. LeR 4 was ordered to attack with all forces simultaneously both targets and repeat the attack as quickly as possible.

LeLv 42 and 44 attacked at seven in the morning the river Vodla with 12 Blenheims and then again at eleven with the same number. The latter mission was protected by six Brewsters from Hirvas. As a whole the results were modest, even if no enemy air opposition or flak were observed above the targets. The board yard was set on fire and a few hits were scored on the barges. The unit bombing prevented accurate aiming and the incendiaries dropped in the water had hardly any effect.

On 8 and 9 July all squadrons of LeR 4 participated in the fighting over Someri. On the latter day the only visible damage caused by LeR 4 was gained, when *ev.luutn*. Birger Gabrielsson led seven Blenheims of LeLv 44 in an attack on a gunboat south of Someri. One hit was observed on the stern of the gunboat. Moscow class gunboat "*Kama*" received a hit from *ltm*. Unto Oksala, becoming heavily damaged, but did not sink and was towed away. Six Brewsters escorted over the target.

In the town of Segesha, located on the west bank of lake Uikujärvi, was a gun factory, sulphuric acid factory and cellulose mill plus a power plant. These, in addition to a noteworthy air base, were to become regular targets of LeR 4. The next blow of the whole regiment was carried out on 31 August, this time on the air base. In all 22 bombers took off headed for the target. LeLv 44 attacked in the lead with *ev.luutn*. Gabrielsson's eight Blenheims. The bombs exploded evenly on

BL-109 of 1/LeLv 42 on a stop at Nurmoila on 23 August 1942. The flight leader, kapt. *Niilo Hakala, flew a photographic mission beyond the River Svir. The machine spent almost three years in repair after a bad accident and was delivered to the unit on 6 February 1942, in brand new Warpaint applied on 4 January 1942. (Kyösti Karhila)*

BL-155 of 3/LeLv 44 was the mount of the flight leader, luutn. Jouko Saarinen. It is seen here at Onttola in summer 1942. The nose carried the flight badge, a bomb carrying bird. (Kari Stenman coll.)

BL-115 of 1/LeLv 44 returning to Onttola from a bombing mission to Segesha air base on 24 November 1942, piloted by the flight leader, kapt. Erkki Itävuori. (SA-kuva)

the target, where several fires were lit. Then LeLv 42 bombed with *kapt.* Hakala's three Blenheims, causing west of the airfield a 500 m long fire and east of the field a 200 m long fire.

At the beginning of 1943 LeLv 42 had five and LeLv 44 eight serviceable Blenheims.

The bombardment of Segesha armament factories had been postponed several times, but a regiment attack was made on 19 February 1943. It was decided to carry this out at 17 hours by 18 aircraft of four squadrons. LeLv 42 bombed with *luutn.* Jorma Turpeinen's four Blenheims at 16.55 and made a direct hit on a large factory building, resulting in a strong explosion and fire. LeLv 44 attacked with *luutn.* Tauno Iisalo's five Blenheims, bombing at 17.05 and scoring hits in the target area, where a large fire was lit.

On 20 February LeLv 44 transferred their remaining four Blenheims to LeLv 42, which was for the rest of the year the only operational Blenheim outfit. During the Continuation War LeLv 44 had flown with the Blenheims 739 sorties. Ten Blenheims were lost, two of which were missing in action, two shot down by fighters and one by flak, in addition to five destroyed in flying accidents or due to technical failure. A total of 26 airmen were killed. The rear gunners claimed one Soviet fighter shot down.

On 17 March the first squadron attack by LeLv 42 was made under the lead of *maj.* Olavi Lumiala, when eight Blenheims bombed in eastern Karelia the barracks area at Sumskaya and the nearby Jeljärvi station. One warehouse exploded and another caught fire.

On 20 August LeR 4 flew a joint bombing mission targeting the Eastern Karelian village of Lehto, where a large partisan supply and training base was located. Thirty-one bombers went to

the target escorted by twelve Moranes. *Kapt*. Hakala's five Blenheims of LeLv 42 bombed at 03.28 hitting the target.

The evening of September 17 seemed like a good moment for LeR 4 to carry out the long planned attack on Lavansaari. It was to be bombed with 30 planes between 20.15–21.55 and again between 03.00–04.00. Haze appeared over the Gulf of Finland, causing an hour's delay and expectations of a recall, which did not appear. Four Blenheims of LeLv 42 led by *luutn*. Huhtala bombed at 21.34, from 3,200 m. Due to haze no confirmation of hits could be made, but some fires were started by the bombs. Three other Blenheims of LeLv 42 were led by *kapt*. Ahokas, bombing at 21.37, also from 3,200 m. No confirmation of hits could be made because of heavy haze and intense AA fire, which downed one aircraft. The second strike was called off.

During the fall, the State Aircraft Factory finished a 30 plane series of Blenheims, giving LeLv 48 a new set of planes, deliveries commencing on 11 November, with ten more during the month. The unit was declared operational on 18 December 1943

On 1 January 1944 LeLv 42 possessed 16 Blenheims and LeLv 48 another 13. On 14 February the squadron abbreviation was changed to PLeLv, numbering remaining the same.

The ADD, long distance bombing unit of the Russians, bombed Helsinki in force on three nights in February. The planes flew from fields around Leningrad, where the Finnish reconnaissance missions had noted dozens of planes on each site. The fields were fully lit at take-off and landing times, and thus were good targets for bombing.

On 2 March LeR 4 was ordered to bomb Russian airfields on the Karelian Isthmus with all squadrons. Finnish bombers were to join the returning Russian bomber fleets and bomb the fields,

BL-155 (nearest) and BL-161 of 3/LeLv 42 at Värtsilä on 11 December 1943. The former arrived with its unit a fortnight earlier, being repaired at the factory, which painted the undersides in DN-väri on 2 October 1943. (SA-kuva)

BL-161 and BL-168 of 3/LeLv 42 ready for a training flight from Värtsilä on 11 December 1943. The strength of the flights had risen to five aircraft due to the completion of the V series aircraft, of which BL-161 was the first one, rolling out on 19 July 1943. (SA-kuva)

A training day at T-LeLv 17 base at Luonetjärvi during the last week of March 1944. Above BL-111 is landing, in the middle BL-179 in towed to the runway and below BL-115 is taxiing prior to take-off. All aircraft have the regulation DN-väri undersides. (SA-kuva)

usually well lit, at landing times. Aerial photography of 6 March showed the following: Kasimovo, 31 Li-2 and 3 Il-2: Shuvalovo, 12 Boston, 3 DF, 2 Il-2, 2 I-153, 1 1/1 and 1 SB: Levashovo 54 Li-2 and 9 Yak-1: Gorskaya 31 Li-2 and 15 Yak-1. Konnajalahti was empty.

On 9 March LeR 4 was given a chance to infiltrate an ADD bombing mission returning from Tallinn. Over the Gulf of Finland, the Finns joined the formations and flew to their bases. PLeLv 42 followed the Russians to Gorskaya with five Blenheims led by *luutn.* Timo Autio. Four planes bombed Gorskaya at 21.30–21.32. Hits were recorded in the plane revetments and shelters at the south and north-west sides of the field. One plane bombed Levashovo at 21.34 hitting the row of planes on the west side of the field. Two planes burned, a huge explosion on the north side of the field was seen, with massive smoke and fire, visible at 70 kms. PLeLv 48 followed the Russians to Levashovo with *kapt.* Hakala's four planes. At 21.37 one plane bombed Levashovo and three planes bombed the only lit field, Gorskaya, at 21.40–21.45. Hits were observed on the north side of the field, with five planes burning, and on the south-west side two planes burned and one storage hut exploded.

These extremely successful attacks led to the sacking of the ADD commanding general and downgrading the elite outfit to a regular air army.

On 30 March LeR 4 bombed Mergino field, south of the mouth of the River Svir, with 31 planes after seven in the evening. Prior to this attack, PLeLv 42 sent two Blenheims to mark the target with illumination bombs. The bombs of 17 Blenheims of PLeLv 42 and PLeLv 48 did hit the target area and a few fires were lit. Due to haze, no accurate assessment was possible.

On 3 April LeR 4 concentrated 34 planes for an attack on the airfield at Kähy, north-east of Leningrad. Aerial reconnaissance had found 57 planes there the day before. PLeLv 48 bombed with 10 Blenheims led by *kapt.* Hakala. Hits were observed in target area on the south-west side of the airfield. Many fires started in the target area and also east of the field. Next up was PLeLv 42, also with 10 planes led by *luutn.* Tauno Kangas. Hits were recorded on the target and four fires observed.

After the spring thaw was over, the airfield of Mergino at the mouth of the River Svir became a target once more, on 19 May. LeR 4 took off with 42 planes, 41 of which bombed the base right after midnight. This was the biggest number of planes the regiment ever managed to get to the target. PLeLv 42 bombed with *luutn.* Kangas's 13 Blenheims, hitting the target. Large numbers of incendiary bombs landed on the north end of the runway. Big explosions and large fires were observed at the target. PLeLv 48 came last to the scene, led by *maj.* Ahtiainen and his 12 Blenheims. The bomb strikes were in the target area, with a large even area of fire noted. No accurate assessment of hits could be made due to dusk and heavy haze.

A massive Soviet attack commenced on 9 June on the Karelian Isthmus, supported by the Soviet 13th Air Army with more than 1,100 planes, and the left flank was protected by 220 planes from the Baltic Fleet Air Force. These warplanes were concentrated on a 20 kilometre strip of land on the eastern Gulf of Finland.

LeR 4 was given an order to prepare for an all-out attack on the Karelian Isthmus. To avoid losses and spare the sparse resources, the regiment ordered attacks to take place primarily at night.

On 12 June LeR 4 performed its first combined bombing in the blocking battles fought on the Karelian Isthmus. The 38 planes, including 17 Blenheims from PLeLv 42 and PLeLv 48, had tanks and columns on the Kivennapa-Mainila road as targets.

On 16 June LeR 4 targeted a naval convoy of 36 ships south of Koivisto, heading west-north-west. Six large ships were part of the convoy. The regiment sent 30 planes to attack at 15.39, and caused the convoy to disperse and issue a smokescreen. This did not impede bombing, which was performed in small groups and single planes. PLeLv 48 bombed with *kapt.* Turpeinen and his five Blenheims, hitting the middle ships, setting fire to two ships. PLeLv 42 bombed with *kapt.* Kangas and his 13 Blenheims ,scoring hits across two major ships, one giving smoke after a direct hit. Hits straddled an escort destroyer and a transport. Other hits were seen in the middle of the convoy. Bombing caused the convoy to disperse and some ships even turned back east. Eighteen Messerschmitts escorted the bombers.

On 19 June just before midnight LeR 4 took off with 35 planes, including 13 Blenheims, to attack the Humaljoki estuary, where an amphibious enemy fleet was approaching. Dusk made it impossible for some planes to see the ships, and eight planes bombed secondary targets on the coast. The bombs dropped on the convoy fell in the middle of the ships, and some ships ceased to fire AA after the bombing.

On 21 June it was decreed that *Lentorykmentti* 4 was to operate in the Viipuri-Tali area and to perform also daylight attacks regardless of losses.

On June 22, after midnight, LeR 4 sent 36 planes, half of them being Blenheims, to bomb artillery batteries at Häyry east of Viipuri. In the evening LeR 4 attacked with 27 planes; horizontal bombers went for the tanks seen on the Tali-Mannikkala road. No hits were scored on the bridges but the timing of the attack was perfect and it caused much havoc and confusion among the Russian troops about to attack. Four detachments of six Messerschmitts each flew escort.

On 26 June PLeLv 42 bombed enemy ground forces at the Tali station with 15 planes, led by *kapt*. Kangas. Hits were seen at the target area. *Kapt*. Siirilä and his 11 BL bombers of PLeLv 28 bombed the Tali station and bridges at the same time, escorted by Messerschmitts.

On 29 June shortly before midnight *maj*. Kepsu took seventeen Blenheims of PLeLv 42 to bomb two road bridges west of Kärstilänjärvi. Hits were obtained near the bridges but they remained unbroken. *Maj*. Esko Ahtiainen led seven Blenheims of PLeLv 48 to bomb Tali. Eight Messerschmitts flew escort.

On the last day of June LeR 4 sent 40 planes to bomb enemy groupings, vehicles, and tanks at the Portinhoikka junction. The formation included 23 Blenheims and was escorted by 19 Messerschmitts. This 59 plane detachment was the biggest ever Finnish formation during the entire war.

On 1 July early in the morning, LeR 4 went once more to attack Portinhoikka with 37 bombers, with 24 Blenheims and a 12-plane Messerschmitt escort managing to get to the target. A strong explosion was seen in the target area.

Two days later early in the morning, LeR 4 attacked Russian infantry, tanks and artillery positions in the Vakkila-Ihantala area with 38 planes, including 23 Blenheims. A strong explosion was seen at the target. Twelve Messerschmitts flew escort.

On 4 July early in the morning, LeR 4 bombed a naval convoy with 37 planes while the convoy moved under cover of smoke at Tuppuransaari. Two direct hits on ships were obtained and there was also a forceful explosion seen in the middle of the artificial smoke, out of which a high column of smoke arose. Twenty-three Blenheims participated in this attack.

One of ten Blenheim IVs of the VI series was BL-198, which was delivered to 2/PLeLv 42 on 2 April 1944, usually flown by the flight leader kapt. Aimo Huhtala. Here seen at Immola soon after arrival. It also features the new VL-designed carburettor dust filters on both sides of the cowling, installed to all new V and VI series bombers and retro-fitted to most others. The national insignia is the subdued type, as issued on 12 January 1944. (Paavo Saari)

By 5 July the Russian advance at Tali and Ihantala stalled because of ferocious defence by the Finns. Now it was time for the last but one all-regiment bombing mission to Tali. Twenty-one Blenheims, took off to bomb the artillery positions with the whole LeR 4 force of 36 bombers.

In the evening an attack by 34 planes with 20 Blenheims was carried out, targeting tanks and artillery at Äyräpää. The bombs hit concentrated Russian forces. A strong explosion was seen and many fires were lit.

On 8 July the bombings of Äyräpää and Vuosalmi were the peak of LeR 4 activities in the summer of 1944, as it attempted to stem the Russian operations by focused bombing attacks. In the morning the targets were tanks, infantry groups, and artillery positions at Äyräpää. Twenty Blenheims and 11 other bombers were escorted by eleven Messerschmitts.

On 14 July LeR 4 went out on full force attacks three times, early in the morning to Käsnäselkä on the north-east shores of Lake Ladoga with 34 bombers, then in the day to Äyräpää also with 34 planes, and in the evening to Pitkäranta on the north-east side of Lake Ladoga with 32 planes.

On 15 July LeR 4 flew regimental bombing efforts three times once more. Early in the morning the target for 32 planes was the river crossing at Äyräpää, at noon there was a 26 plane attack on artillery positions at Nietjärvi behind Lake Ladoga, and in the evening another attack by 27 planes flew to bomb the Vuosalmi bridgehead. Two flights of Messerschmitts escorted the planes over the Isthmus, and on the Nietjärvi mission a flight of Brewsters and Curtiss flew top cover.

In the early morning of 16 July, PLeLv 42 sent *maj.* Kepsu with 16 Blenheims to bomb tank formations at Nietjärvi north-east of Lake Ladoga, and a large fire was seen as a result.

On 18 July the Russian attacks had subsided at Vuosalmi. They had managed a breach to the north of River Vuoksi some five kilometres wide and two kilometres deep. The morning regimental bombing of Vuosalmi was decided to be executed at an altitude a couple kilometres higher than usual. Thirty bombers and 16 Messerschmitts took off to carry out the mission. PLeLv 48 flew with *kapt.* Olavi Siirilä's five Blenheims, releasing the bombs at 06.04 on the assigned target area from 4,700 m. *Kapt.* Huhtala led his 14 Blenheims of PLeLv 42 bombing at 06.07.30–06.08 from 4,000 m, hitting the target.

In the afternoon, 24 planes renewed the attack with a 16 plane escort. These were the last sorties to Vuosalmi, where the enemy's offensive had been blocked. The centre of gravity shifted now to the areas behind Lake Ladoga, where the last decisive battles of the Continuation War were fought.

Early in the morning of 22 July LeR 4 bombed with 34 planes the troops and artillery positions between Lake Vegarus and Lake Kollaa. A sizeable explosion was seen at the target. Five Moranes escorted the bombers.

On 26 July in the evening LeR 4 sent 34 planes to bomb artillery and vehicle concentrations between Kollaa and Näätäoja, hitting the crowded target. A pair of Messerschmitts and six Curtisses covered the mission.

Next evening LeR 4 attacked artillery and equipment with 30 planes at Tolvajärvi. Six Curtisses flew top cover.

Early in the morning of 28 July LeR 4 sent 30 planes to bomb artillery positions at the Kollaanjärvi-Näätäoja area. A dozen Moranes and Curtisses flew escort.

On 1 August 27 level bombers of LeR 4 attacked in the early hours the bridges at Vuonteleenjärvi. Squadrons were delayed and missed their thresholds; initially only one escort fighter took off from Värtsilä, and finally three Messerschmitts attempted to perform the escort duty. Large gaps formed in the bomber train and on the return leg Russian fighters managed to get at the bombers, shooting down two PLeLv 42 Blenheims.

Early in the morning of 4 August LeR 4 attacked with 17 Blenheim the Russian columns moving along the Jakunvaara-Salmijärvi road. At the unloading spot of the troops a strong explosion and resultant smoke were seen. In the evening LeR 4 bombed a column on the Salmijärvi-Moisionvaara road. Nineteen Blenheims scored direct hits on vehicles and the infantry, and many fires were lit. A pair of Messerschmitts flew escort.

On 9 August the last regimental bombing effort was to attack the Suojärvi station with 30 planes. The goal was to disrupt the retreat of moving equipment. The planes went in two waves, escorted by six Messerschmitts. PLeLv 48 arrived with kapt. Siirilä leading six Blenheims, bombing at 21.20 from 3,700 m and hitting the target. PLeLv 42 ended regimental bombardments with *maj.* Kepsu's thirteen Blenheims bombing at 21.45 from 3,800 m, also hitting the target area, where fires were seen from previous bombings.

On 25 August the last mission of LeR4 was flown when a Blenheim of PLeLv 48 photographed the Tali-Sorvali-Koivisto roads with four Messerschmitts escorting.

On 4 September the commander of the Air Force ordered the air regiments to tell squadrons to cease fighting at 07.00. A ceasefire commenced and two weeks later it was confirmed by the Moscow Armistice.

PLeLv 42 used Blenheims during the whole Continuation War, performing a total of 1,605 missions. Twenty-two planes were lost, four to enemy fighters and six to flak, while three were missing in action and seven were destroyed accidentally. Forty-nine airmen were killed, and two were made POW. Two enemy fighters were shot down by rear gunners.

BL-155 of 3/PLeLv 42 at Onttola on 22 June 1944. Behind is BL-156. These bombers had the VLS wooden propeller instead of the usual de Havilland metal propeller. After the early hours bombardment of Tali the squadron landed at Onttola and flew back to Naarajärvi in the afternoon. At the controls of BL-155 on these sorties was vänr. Ville Niskanen. (SA-kuva)

BL-199 was the mount of 2/PLeLv 42 leader kapt. *Erkki Palosuo. Seen here being re-fuelled by manpower at Onttola on 22 June 1944. Palosuo's plane was easily identified by its white propeller spinners, rather than the more common black or olive green ones. (SA-kuva)*

The main equipment of PLeLv 48 was Blenheims from 1 November 1943. A total of 413 sorties were flown. Losses totalled seven Blenheims (flak three, enemy fighters two, enemy bombing two, accidents one). Eight aircrew members were killed.

War in Lapland

The agreement of cessation of hostilities between Finland and the Soviet Union included a requirement that German troops in Finland were to be either stripped of arms, or expelled from the country, by 15 September 1944.

On September 4 the Air Force set up the Special Staff Sarko, with *ev.* Olavi Sarko commanding, in view of the air war in Lapland. On 15 September LeR 2 and LeR 4 were ordered to prepare to participate in the war in Lapland.

The real action began when the Finns made a surprise landing in the rear of the Germans in Tornio on October 1.

The first offensive mission of LeR 4 was to bomb on 2 October German troops, vehicles and columns which were retreating along the main roads to Rovaniemi. The squadrons took off at intervals from their bases some 500 kms away. *Maj.* Ahtiainen led the seven Blenheims of PLeLv 48 as they bombed columns on the Ala-Portimojärvi-Rovaniemi road at 16.40–16.47. At 5 pm PLeLv 42 bombed with *kapt.* Kangas and his 13 Blenheims, targets being marching columns on the Ala-Portimojärvi-Rovaniemi road. Flak shot down one aircraft.

All bombings were from less than 1,000 m altitude, and the Finns reported many direct hits on columns, but the Germans considered the damage minimal. On the whole, the northern bombing offensive remained at nuisance level, because the German radar-controlled and very intense flak shot through the clouds and forced bombing altitude to be elevated, which in turn reduced the accuracy.

On 6 October PLeLv 42 possessed 14 Blenheims and PLeLv 48 another six Blenheims for operations in Lapland. Four days later LeR 4 bombed German troops with 23 planes along the road between Rovaniemi and Ranua.

On 21 October PLeLv 42 sent *kapt.* Kangas and his nine Blenheims and PLeLv 48 sent *maj.* Ahtiainen with four planes to bomb troops on the Kittilä-Muonio road. The weather was good and bombing occurred out of the reach of light flak, and troop columns were sent into disarray.

On 16 November PLeLv 42 sent *kapt.* Huhtala and his nine Blenheims to bomb German troops en route from Palojoensuu towards Kilpisjärvi.

Next day the entire LeR 4 attacked German troops as well as camp and storage areas in the region between Kaaresuvanto and Suikero. *Maj.* Kepsu bombed troops retreating towards Kilpisjärvi

BL-175 of 1/PLeLv 48 at Vesivehmaa in early September 1944. Luutn. Kullervo Virtanen usually flew this aircraft on photographic missions. This flight was denoted by white propeller spinner tips. The light patch on the nose is the squadron emblem, the red devils of Onttola. (Kullervo Virtanen)

BL-190 of 3/PLeLv 48 on the platform at Immola in late April 1944. The regular pilot was luutn. Leo Töllikkö. This flight had red propeller spinner tips. Also the flight emblem shows to good advantage on the nose. (Kaarlo Juurikas)

Due to plane shortages, TLeLv 12 received from PLeLv 48 two Blenheims for its 3rd Flight. BL-184 arrived on 19 June and BL-181 on 3 July 1944. The planes were returned on 10 October 1944. Both are seen here at Onttola in August 1944. (Lauri Kippo)

on the riverside road with seven PLeLv 42 Blenheims. *Kapt.* Siirilä bombed a camp area at Suonttavaara with five PLeLv 48 Blenheims.

On 18 November PLeLv 48 flew its last war mission when *kapt.* Ranta and his four Blenheims bombed artillery positions at Palojoensuu with hits in the target area.

On 4 December 1944 the Air Force was returned to its peacetime strength. The squadrons were renumbered and PLeLv 42 became PLeLv 41. PLeLv 48 was disbanded.

On 2 Januaruy 1945 PLeLv 41 flew its last mission of the war as it bombed a group of barracks with two Blenheims at Ropijärvi along the Kilpisjärvi road.

The Lapland War lasted for 183 days, only on 43 was the weather good enough for flying. PLeLv 42 took off for 106 sorties and PLeLv 48 for 51. Three bombers were lost, and four crew members were killed and two more taken POW.

S/n	C/n	Delivered	Struck off charge	Remarks	Flying Hours
BL-104	I/1	29 Jul 1937	20 May 1942	W/o Tiiksjärvi 5 Mar 1942	396.25
BL-105	I/2	29 Jul 1937	16 Aug 1942	W/o Höytiäinen 26 Jun 1942	373.15
BL-106	I/3	9 Dec 1937	4 Dec 1958	W/o Rovaniemi 20 Mar 1957	2005.40
BL-107	I/4	23 Dec 1937	5 Oct 1943	W/o Korpiselkä 23 Aug 1943	488.25
BL-108	I/5	23 Dec 1937	11 Mar 1940	W/o Siikakangas 28 Jan 1940	174.20
BL-109	I/6	25 Feb 1938	9 Sep 1952	Last flight 19 Oct 1945	611.10
BL-110	I/9	2 Mar 1938	11 Mar 1940	W/o Raulampi 1 Dec 1939	158.20
BL-111	I/7	25 Feb 1938	1 Oct 1952	Last flight 15 Feb 1946	771.30
BL-112	I/8	26 Feb 1938	11 Mar 1940	W/o Riihilampi 6 Jan 1940	217.25
BL-113	I/10	30 Jun 1938	12 Apr 1940	W/o Lake Ladoga 18 Feb 1940	97.25
BL-114	I/11	30 Jun 1938	10 Aug 1941	W/o Suojärvi 13 Jul 1941	259
BL-115	I/12	8 Jul 1938	7 Sep 1952	Last flight 11 Sep 1948	789.15
BL-116	I/13	8 Jul 1938	20 Sep 1941	W/o Vuoksela 14 Aug 1941	487.45
BL-117	I/14	20 Jul 1938	20 Sep 1941	W/o Sortavala 20 Aug 1941	273.25
BL-118	I/15	20 Jul 1938	31 Dec 1941	W/o Onttola 3 Nov 1941	368.30
BL-119	I/18	27 Jul 1938	12 Apr 1940	W/o Syskyjärvi 26 Feb 1940	209.10
BL-120	I/17	27 Jul 1938	9 Sep 1952	Last flight 6 Jul 1946	986
BL-121	I/16	27 Jul 1938	11 Mar 1940	W/o Lake Ladoga 19 Jan 1940	191.45
BL-122	III/	21 Jan 1940	9 May 1940	W/o Vilaniemi 7 Mar 1940	28.30
BL-123	III/	21 Jan 1940	11 Mar 1940	W/o Luonetjärvi 14 Feb 1940	
BL-124	III/	21 Jan 1940	26 Jul 1941	W/o Vahviala 1 Jul 1941	
BL-125	III/	31 May 1940	30 Jan 1941	W/o Laukaa 18 Dec 1940	83.15
BL-126	III/	21 Jan 1940	6 May 1940	W/o Utti 29 Feb 1940	22.55
BL-127	III/			W/o Norway 18 Jan 1940	
BL-128	III/	21 Jan 1940	26 Oct 1940	W/o Luonetjärvi 4 Oct 1940	185.55
BL-129	III/	21 Jan 1940	9 Sep 1952	Last flight 18 Jul 1946	775.15
BL-130	III/	21 Jan 1940	26 Jul 1941	W/o Vahviala 1 Jul 1941	
BL-131	III/	21 Jan 1940	15 Jan 1941	W/o Luonetjärvi 27 Nov 1940	184.10
BL-132	III/	21 Jan 1940	23 Nov 1942	W/o Peninsaari 29 Jun 1942	143.20
BL-133	III/	21 Jan 1940	25 May 1940	W/o Viipurinlahti 10 Mar 1940	48.40
BL-134	IV/	26 Feb 1940	10 Aug 1941	W/o Lotinanpelto 13 Jul 1941	402.25
BL-135	IV/	26 Feb 1940	9 Jul 1943	W/o Luonetjärvi 9 Jul 1943	816.55
BL-136	IV/	26 Feb 1940	20 Sep 1941	W/o Tiiksjärvi 13 Aug 1941	397.50
BL-137	IV/	26 Feb 1940	27 Sep 1941	W/o Värtsilä 3 Sep 1941	288.15
BL-138	IV/	26 Feb 1940	13 Jun 1944	W/o Luonetjärvi 9 Mar 1944	890.40

Blenheim BL-120 of 2/PLeLv 48 at Vesivehmaa in early September 1944, prior to the removal of the yellow eastern front markings. Vänr. Jaakko Huhti was the regular pilot of this bomber. The aircraft was repainted during damage repair at the factory on 12 July 1944. (Finnish Aviation Museum)

BL-139	IV/	26 Feb 1940	15 Aug 1941	W/o Säämäjärvi 21 Jul 1941	527
BL-140	IV/	26 Feb 1940	30 Nov 1943	W/o Luonetjärvi 18 Aug 1943	981.45
BL-141	IV/	26 Feb 1940	10 Aug 1941	W/o Lake Ladoga 21 Jul 1941	499.35
BL-142	IV/	26 Feb 1940	9 Sep 1952	Last flight 15 Aug 1946	720.25
BL-143	IV/	26 Feb 1940	6 Nov 1941	W/o Lake Onega 2 Oct 1941	641.30
BL-144	IV/	26 Feb 1940	9 May 1940	W/o Viipurinlahti 7 Mar 1940	
BL-145	IV/	26 Feb 1940	15 Aug 1941	W/o Jyväskylä 25 Jul 1941	374.15
BL-146	II/1	14 Jun 1941	27 Sep 1941	W/o Lahdenpohja 7 Aug 1941	22.30
BL-147	II/2	1 Aug 1941	20 May 1942	W/o Loviisa 27 Mar 1942	126.25
BL-148	II/3	7 Aug 1941	22 Feb 1943	W/o Immola 6 Jan 1943	105
BL-149	II/4	25 Aug 1941	20 May 1942	W/o Loviisa 27 Mar1942	92.40
BL-150	II/5	4 Sep 1941	16 Jul 1943	W/o Sumeri 23 May 1943	231.35
BL-151	II/6	16 Sep 1941	9 Sep 1952	Last flight 5 Jan 1945	320.25
BL-152	II/7	29 Sep 1941	9 Jan 1943	W/o Värtsilä 7 Nov 1941	101.45
BL-153	II/8	7 Oct 1941	30 Jan 1942	W/o Peljaki 9 Dec 1941	25.50
BL-154	II/9	16 Oct 1941	20 May 1942	W/o Varbinitsy 15 Apr 1942	74.45
BL-155	II/10	26 Oct 1941	9 Sep 1952	Last flight 13 Dec 1946	311.25
BL-156	II/11	19 Oct 1941	9 Mar 1945	W/o Ounasjoki 18 Oct 1944	264.25
BL-157	II/12	16 Nov 1941	20 May 1942	W/o Varbinitsy 15 Apr 1942	59.55
BL-158	II/13	25 Nov 1941	26 Sep 1944	W/o Tohmajärvi 1 Aug 1944	353.35
BL-159	II/14	12 Dec 1941	20 May 1942	W/o Varbinitsy 15 Apr 1942	33.20
BL-160	II/15	9 Jan 1942	26 Sep 1944	W/o Korpiselkä 1 Aug 1944	295.50
BL-161	V/1	19 Jul 1943	11 Sep 1946	W/o Luonetjärvi 18 Jul 1946	200+
BL-162	V/2	28 Jul 1943	2 Jan 1950	W/o Kauhava 12 Sep 1946	244.10
BL-163	V/3	6 Aug 1943	26 Oct 1943	W/o Lacvansaari 17 Sep 1943	7.40
BL-164	V/4	11 Aug 1943	26 Oct 1943	W/o Jaakkima 17 Sep 1943	15.30
BL-165	V/5	20 Aug 1943	11 Dec 1952	Last flight 18 May 1946	209.55
BL-166	V/6	27 Aug 1943	10 Jan 1946	W/o Hirvensalmi 21 Nov 1945	166.45
BL-167	V/7	31 Aug 1943	9 Sep 1952	W/o Hyvinkää 26 Jun 1948	324
BL-168	V/8	3 Sep 1943	9 Sep 1952	Last flight 26 Mar 1947	212.45
BL-169	V/9	6 Sep 1943	9 Sep 1952	Last flight 29 Nov 1946	248.10
BL-170	V/10	18 Sep 1943	2 Sep 1944	W/o Lemetti 15 Jul 1944	39.50
BL-171	V/11	25 Sep 1943	9 Sep 1952	Last flight 14 Sep 1948	334.30
BL-172	V/12	30 Sep 1943	16 Sep 1947	W/o Kauhava 20 Jun 1947	319.50

BL-173	V/13	6 Oct 1943	16 Mar 1959	Last flight 10 Apr 1958	712.35
BL-174	V/14	7 Oct 1943	26 Sep 1944	W/o Onttola 8 Aug 1944	116.45
BL-175	V/15	12 Oct 1943	9 Sep 1952	Last flight 14 Sep 1948	499
BL-176	V/16	13 Oct 1943	9 Sep 1952	Last flight 26 May 1948	315.45
BL-177	V/17	16 Oct 1943	30 Jun 1947	W/o Rissala 24 May 1947	140.25
BL-178	V/18	18 Oct 1943	9 Sep 1952	W/o Luonetjärvi 21 Aug 1948	467.45
BL-179	V/19	22 Oct 1943	9 Sep 1952	Last flight 17 Mar 1948	470.50
BL-180	V/20	23 Oct 1943	20 Feb 1945	W/o Laukaa 11 Oct 1944	279.05
BL-181	V/21	1 Nov 1943	9 Sep 1952	Last flight 23 Nov 1944	123.20
BL-182	V/22	1 Nov 1943	11 Dec 1952	W/o Turku 5 Apr 1945	92.05
BL-183	V/23	2 Nov 1943	21 Apr 1944	W/o Laukaa 11 Apr 1944	35.15
BL-184	V/24	3 Nov 1943	9 Sep 1952	Last flight 13 Sep 1948	167.25
BL-185	V/25	8 Nov 1943	26 Sep 1944	W/o Nuijamaa 27 Jun 1944	68.40
BL-186	V/27	13 Nov 1943	2 Sep 1944	W/o Tali 27 Jun 1944	55.55
BL-187	V/26	16 Nov 1943	9 Sep 1952	Last flight 4 Feb 1947	219.10
BL-188	V/28	16 Nov 1943	9 Sep 1952	W/o Luonetjärvi 7 Jun 1948	427.30
BL-129	V/29	24 Nov 1943	26 Sep 1944	W/o Onttola 8 Aug 1944	111
BL-190	V/30	24 Nov 1943	7 Jun 1945	W/o Lapland 5 Oct 1944	97.55
BL-196	VI/1	26 Feb 1944	9 Sep 1952	Last flight 14 Sep 1948	320.20
BL-197	VI/2	28 Feb 1944	6 Oct 1958	Last flight 20 Oct 1953	1,137.10
BL-198	VI/4	17 Mar 1944	11 Dec 1944	W/o Ylimaa 2 Oct 1944	148.25
BL-199	VI/5	2 Apr 1944	16 Mar 1959	Last flight 20 May 1958	707.05
BL-200	VI/3	21 Mar 1944	6 Oct 1958	Last flight 5 Jun 1957	885.15
BL-201	VI/7	29 Mar 1944	9 Sep 1952	Last flight 11 Sep 1948	379.10
BL-202	VI/6	30 Mar 1944	9 Aug 1944	W/o Kivennapa 12 Jun 1944	33.30
BL-203	VI/8	11 Apr 1944	4 May 1946	W/o Luonetjärvi 23 Feb 1945	84.40
BL-204	VI/10	15 Apr 1944	9 Sep 1952	Last flight 13 Sep 1948	397
BL-205	VI/9	14 Apr 1944	9 Sep 1952	Last flight 11 Sep 1948	302.40

The aircrews of 3/PLeLv 48 at Vesivehmaa in early September 1944. Behind are BL-203 and BL-205. Back row from left: Lampimäki, Lakovuo, Lindqvist, Aromaa, Koskivirta, Ylennysmäki, Tiainen, Pihkala, Hälvä and Saarenketo. Sitting from left: Juva, Aapro, Juurikas, Nieminen, Platan (flight leader), Töllikkö, Kurten, Karikoski and Suninen. (Kaarlo Juurikas)

Bristol Blenheim
Camouflage and markings

The first batch (I series, BL-104–121) of 17 new Blenheims bought from Britain were painted according to the Finnish specifications: upper surfaces and fuselage in Olive Green (*Kenttävihreä*) and undersides in aluminium lacquer. The III series (BL-122–133) of 12 new "long nose" Blenheims, flown to Finland in January 1940, was similarly painted.

The IV series (BL-134–145) arriving in February 1940 consisted of 12 ex-RAF Blenheims, wearing the contemporary British bomber camouflage of Dark Green and Dark Earth upper surfaces with Black underside.

On 30 September 1940 Warpaint was introduced. This consisted of Olive Green and Black upper sides and for metal covered aircraft, aluminium lacquer lower sides. The first Blenheim to receive Warpaint was BL-145 on 28 December 1940, followed by BL-132 on 14 January 1941 and BL-114 one day later. Before the Continuation War five more Blenheims received Warpaint, chronologically BL-137, 106, 116, 134 and 107.

The II series (BL-146–160), built under licence in Finland during the latter half of 1941, was in the Warpaint from the start: upper surfaces Olive Green with broad Black bands and aluminium lacquer lower sides.

By the end of 1941 a further eight of the older Blenheims had received Warpaint: chronologically BL – 143, 140, 105, 117, 111, 118, 129 and 115.

The *DN-väri* was first tried on BL-129 on 19 March 1942 and became officially the underside colour of the warplanes on 7 May 1942, to be applied in the next major overhaul or repair.

The second Blenheim to get DN-väri undersides was BL-142 on 19 June 1942 followed by BL-148 on 21 August 1942. Next year the *DN-väri* was applied chronologically to BL-115, 111, 156, 155 and 158.

The last two batches (BL-161–190 and BL-196–205), built in Finland during the second half of 1943 and first half of 1944, received Warpaint with *DN-väri* undersides. This camouflage was used until the Blenheims were put into temporary storage in September 1948.

BL-106 undergoing fixed ski trials at the factory at Tampere in spring 1938. In the Winter War these skis were used by a few Blenheims flying from primitive outposts on the northern front. The camouflage is the original Olive Green upper surfaces and aluminium lacquer undersides, applied by the Bristol factory. (VL)

BL-138 of 1/LLv 42 collapsed at take-off from Juva on 7 March 1940, when the pilot retracted the landing gear by mistake. This is a IV series machine wearing the British camouflage of Dark Green and Dark Earth with Black undersides. (Finnish Air Force)

Below: BL-104 of 2/LLv 44 was damaged by Soviet fighters at Värtsilä on 8 July 1941. Vänr. Ahti Nousiainen flew the plane often. The Warpaint of Olive Green and Black with aluminium lacquer underside was applied at the factory on 15 April 1941. (Kari Stenman coll.)

Top view of LeLv 48 photoplane BL-129 flying over water in summer 1943. The Warpaint pattern was standard for all except the captured aircraft types, variations being small. (Finnish Air Force)

BL-138 of 2/LeLv 42 taxied into a filled bomb crater at Värtsilä on 16 June 1942 and nosed over. The Warpaint was factory applied on 17 April 1942. (Finnish Air Force)

BL-181 of TLeLv 12 seen at Onttola in August 1944, where the films were brought for developing. This squadron used two Blenheims for photo reconnaissance missions north and north-east of Lake Ladoga. (Lauri Kippo)

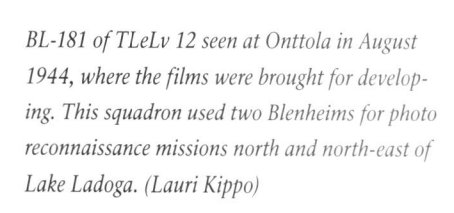

The tail of Salminen's BL-117 showing the number of bombing sorties and his personal skull emblem. The photo dates to shortly before 25 February 1940, when the plane flipped over on an icy runway at Joroinen. (Finnish Aviation Museum)

Bristol Blenheim I, BL-117, ltm. Viljo Salminen, 1/Lentolaivue 44, Joroinen airfield, February 1940. Camouflage colours: upper surfaces Olive Green, under surfaces aluminium dope. Serial British style Black, tail motif White.

BL-117 of LLv 44 slid off the wet runway when landing at Tampere on 4 October 1938. In the Winter War it was the mount of 1/LLv 44 ltm. Viljo Salminen, who later became the first bomber pilot to receive the Mannerheim Cross on 5 November 1941. (VL)

Bristol Blenheim I, BL-111, maj. Erik Stenbäck, commander of Lentolaivue 44, Joroinen airfield, November 1939. Camouflage colours: upper surfaces Olive Green, under surfaces aluminium dope. Serial British style Black.

The landing gear collapsed when LLv 44 CO maj. Erik Stenbäck landed at Luonetjärvi on 23 November 1939. Segments of the white circle of the fuselage insignia have been overpainted with Olive Green during the mobilization for the Winter War. The air force C-in-C disapproved of such tactical measures and gave orders to clean the swastikas. (Finnish Air Force)

Bristol Blenheim I, BL-106, 1/Lentolaivue 44, Kemi airfield, July 1940. Camouflage colours: upper surfaces Olive Green, Dark Grey and Black, under surfaces aluminium dope. Serial British style Black.

BL-106 of 1/LLv 44 went onto its nose while taxiing at Kemi on 12 July 1940. The plane was one of a few which participated in the camouflage tests, leading to the Warpaint a couple of months later. Colours used were Black and Dark Grey over the standard Olive Green. (Finnish Air Force Museum)

Bristol Blenheim I, BL-118, Lentolaivue 44, Kauhava airfield, December 1940. Camouflage colours: upper surfaces Olive Green and Dark Grey, under surfaces aluminium dope. Serial British style Black.

BL-118 of LLv 44 on a visit to Kauhava in late 1940 or early 1941. The plane wears an experimental camouflage of Dark Grey and Black patches on the Olive Green upper surfaces. The fuselage (and probably also wing top) insignia is darkened. (Jorma Nikula)

Bristol Blenheim I, BL-139, Lentolaivue 42, Luonetjärvi airfield, March 1941. Camouflage colours: upper surfaces Olive Green, under surfaces Black. Serial Black.

Blenheim BL-139 of LLv 42 at Luonetjärvi. On 17 January 1941 this machine arrived at the unit after repair, in which all insignia and serials were changed to Finnish standards. The Black lower surfaces have been retained, but the upper surface is regulation Olive Green. (Kari Stenman coll.)

Bristol Blenheim IV, BL-129, luutn. Olavi Siirilä, leader of 3/Lentolaivue 46, Luonetjärvi airfield, March 1940. Camouflage colours: upper surfaces Olive Green, under surfaces aluminium dope. Serial British style Black.

BL-129 of 3/LLv 46 being refuelled at Luonetjärvi on 7 March 1940 before a mission to the Gulf of Viipuri. This plane was one of only three early "long-noses" to see action in the Continuation War and the only one retaining its single-colour upper surfaces, with just the yellow fuselage band and lower wing tips added. (SA-kuva)

Bristol Blenheim I, BL-136, Lentolaivue 42, Luonetjärvi airfield August 1940. Camouflage colours: upper surfaces Dark Green and Dark Earth, under surfaces Black. Serial British style Black.

BL-136 passes low over the Luonetjärvi control tower in August 1940. This 2/LLv 42 plane kept its British camouflage until shot down by Russian flak on 13 August 1941, killing the flight leader, luutn. Niilo Kivi. (Ilmailu)

Bristol Blenheim I, BL-136, luutn. Niilo Kivi, leader of 2/Lentolaivue 42, Joensuu landing ground, July 1941. Camouflage colours: upper surfaces Dark Green and Dark Earth, under surfaces Black. Standard Eastern Front markings Yellow, serial British style Black.

Second lieutenants and nurses in front of BL-136 of 2/LLv 42 at Joensuu in July 1941. The Black underside gives a strong contrast on the light sand. (Armas Eskola)

BL-136 of LLv 42 banks for the photographer in the tower of Luonetjärvi in August 1940. Standard British colours were starting to show wear and tear. The wing insignia is the regulation 4/5th of the chord. (Ilmailu)

Bristol Blenheim I, BL-136, luutn. Niilo Kivi, leader of 2/Lentolaivue 42, Joensuu landing ground, July 1941.

67

Bristol Blenheim I, BL-140, vänr. Kari Grundström, 1/Lentolaivue 42, Värtsilä airfield, September 1941. Camouflage colours: upper surfaces Olive Green and Black, under surfaces Black. Standard Eastern Front markings Yellow, serial British style Black.

Blenheim BL-140 of 1/LLv 42 bellied in at Värtsilä on 29 September 1941, when the port engine quit at take-off. The bomber had unit applied Warpaint during May 1941, retaining its British style serial number. (National Archives)

Bristol Blenheim I. BL-106, luutn. Tauno Iisalo, 1/Lentolaivue 44, Onttola airfield, October 1941. Camouflage colours: upper surfaces Olive Green and Black, under surfaces aluminium dope. Standard Eastern Front markings Yellow, serial Olive Green and Black.

Knight's machine BL-106 of 1/LLv 44 at Onttola in autumn 1941. Future Mannerheim Cross holders Salminen, Oksala, Iisalo and Äijö flew it in turn. (Kari Stenman coll.)

(Main photo) BL-106 of LLv 44 on a visit to Pori in May 1941. The Warpaint was factory applied in March 1941. (Insert) BL-106 served with the 1st Flight in the Continuation war and most missions were flown by luutn. Tauno Iisalo, 36 in total. Seen here at Onttola in September 1941. (Reino Lampelto)

69

Bristol Blenheim II, BL-149, kapt. Erkki Ahmo, leader of 1/Lentolaivue 44, Onttola airfield, October 1941. Camouflage colours: upper surfaces Olive Green and Black, under surfaces aluminium dope. Standard Eastern Front markings Yellow, serial Olive Green and Black.

BL-149 of 1/LLv 44 leader kapt. Erkki Ahmo at Värtsilä landing ground in September 1941. The nose of the plane has an ace of diamonds and a wolverine, translated from his family name. On top is ltm. Unto Oksala in a black pullover, who occasionally flew this plane. (Finnish Air Force)

Bristol Blenheim I, BL-120, luutn. Martti Salo, 2/Lentolaivue 44, Onttola airfield, August 1942. Camouflage colours: upper surfaces Olive Green and Black, under surfaces aluminium dope. Standard Eastern Front markings Yellow, serial Olive Green and Black.

BL-120 of 2/LeLv 44 at Onttola in summer 1942. The regular crew was luutn. Martti Salo as pilot and luutn. Rolf Winqvist as observer. Winqvist was the first observer to receive the Mannerheim Cross, awarded on 1 April 1942. The Warpaint was applied at the factory on 26 April 1942. (Finnish Air Force)

Bristol Blenheim I, BL-111, luutn. Kalevi Heiskanen, 3/Lentolaivue 44, Onttola airfield, September 1942. Camouflage colours: upper surfaces Olive Green and Black, under surfaces aluminium dope. Standard Eastern Front markings Yellow, serial Olive Green and Black.

Frequent pilot of the 3/LeLv 44 machine BL-111 was ltm. Unto Oksala, seen here at left in the cockpit. The unit badge was applied to most of the flight's planes. (Kari Stenman coll.)

BL-111 of 3/LeLv 44 during a visit to Tiiksjärvi on 1 October 1942. Luutn. Sakari Heiskanen photographed in the front-line between Voljärvi and Seesjärvi. (Pauli Ervi)

Bristol Blenheim IV, kapt. Erkki Ahtiainen, leader of ErValok/Lentolaivue 48, Onttola airfield, October 1942. Camouflage colours: upper surfaces Olive Green and Black, under surfaces DN-väri. Standard Eastern Front markings Yellow, serial Olive Green and Black.

Left: BL-129 of LeLv 48 at the end of the 1942 season. This aircraft photographed 40,950 km², mostly beyond Lake Onega and the River Svir. Right: The crew of BL-129 in the 1942 season was, from left, ylik. Yrjö Hammaren, kapt. Esko Ahtiainen and luutn. Lauri Äijö. The fin carries 95 photography mission markers. (Matti Poutvaara)

BL-129 at the beginning of the cartography season at Luonetjärvi in May 1942. This aircraft was the first to received the DN-väri (RLM 65) undersides on 19 March 1942, well before this was approved for combat aircraft on 7 May 1942. (Finnish Air Force)

Bristol Blenheim II, BL-189, Lentovarikko, Tampere airfield, November 1942. Camouflage colours: upper surfaces Olive Green and Black, under surfaces DN-väri. Standard Eastern Front markings Yellow, serial Black.

BL-189 during insignia trials at Tampere in November 1943. The tests showed that this type of insignia was the best, but the headquarters chose the one where the white circle was subdued by light grey or DN-väri. On 13 December 1943 BL-189 was delivered to 2/LeLv 48. (VL)

Bristol Blenheim II, BL-182, vänr. Esa Laukkanen, 3/Pommituslentolaivue 48, Luonetjärvi airfield, April 1944. Camouflage colours: upper surfaces Olive Green and Black, under surfaces DN-väri. Standard Eastern Front markings Yellow, serial Olive Green and Black.

SUODATIN PUHDISTETTAVA 1-2 KÄYTÖN JÄLKEEN

LASKUTELINEEN RENGASPAINE 3,2 IK

HAPEN TÄYTTÖ LIITIN PIDETTÄVÄ VARMASTI PUHTAANA RASVASTA JA LIASTA

SISÄPUOLELLA

KANNUKSEN KIINNITYS JA PYRSTÖOHJAIMET

LASKUTELINEEN RENGASPAINE 3,2 IK

SÄÄTÖLEV OHJAIMET.

SÄÄTÖLEV OHJAIMET.

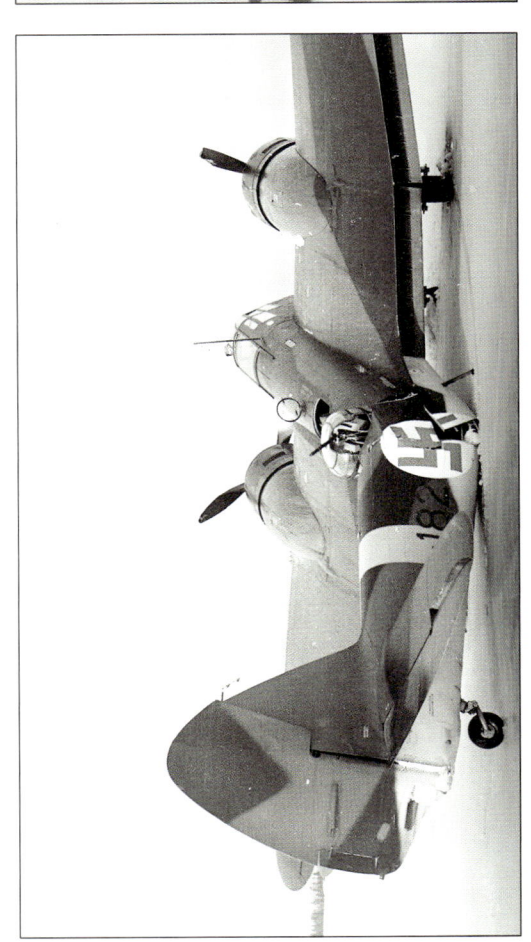

BL-182 of 2/PLeLv 48 had a bad landing at Luonetjärvi on 15 April 1944, hitting the snow bank and breaking the nose and fuselage. The repair took six months. All camouflage, insignia and serials are regulation items as applied at the State Aircraft Factory in October 1943. (SA-kuva)

Bristol Blenheim II, BL-182, vänr. Esa Laukkanen, 3/Pommituslentolaivue 48, Luonetjärvi airfield, April 1944.

SÄÄTÖLEV
OHJAIMET.

BL-182
x 3

KANNUKSEN
KIINNITYS JA
PYRSTÖOHJAIMET

SÄÄTÖLEV
OHJAIMET.

LASKUTELINEEN
RENGASPAINE 3,2 IK

ÄLÄ KOSKE
KEHÄANTENNIIN

ÄLÄ ASTU LEVYLLE

SUODATIN
PUHDISTETTAVA
1-2 KÄYTÖN
JÄLKEEN

LASKUTELINEEN
RENGASPAINE 3,2 IK

BL-182 of 2/PLeLv 48 landing at Luonetjärvi on 5 April 1944. The demarcation line between the top and bottom colours was more angular in V and VI series Blenheims. The lower surfaces are in regulation DN-väri. (SA-kuva)

Bristol Blenheim II, BL-182, vänr. Esa Laukkanen, 3/Pommituslentolaivue 48, Luonetjärvi airfield, April 1944.

ÄLÄ ASTU LEVYLLE

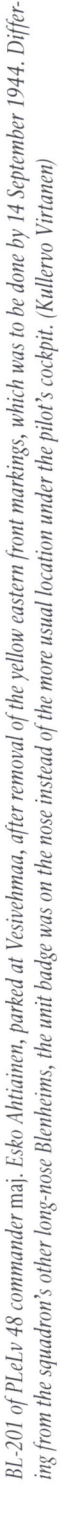

Bristol Blenheim IV, BL-201, maj. Erkki Ahtiainen, commander of Pommituslentolaivue 48, Vesivehmaa airfield, September 1944. Camouflage colours: upper surfaces Olive Green and Black, under surfaces DN-väri. Serial Olive Green and Black.

BL-201 of PLeLv 48 commander maj. Esko Ahtiainen, parked at Vesivehmaa, after removal of the yellow eastern front markings, which was to be done by 14 September 1944. Differing from the squadron's other long-nose Blenheims, the unit badge was on the nose instead of the more usual location under the pilot's cockpit. (Kullervo Virtanen)

Bristol Blenheim IV, BL-129, kapt. Aaro Melasniemi, Valok/Lentolaivue 48, Onttola airfield, August 1943. Camouflage colours: upper surfaces Olive Green and Black, under surfaces DN-väri. Serial Olive Green and Black.

BL-129 of LeLv 48 taxiing at Onttola in summer 1943. The aircraft was used in cartography missions. The nose had two cameras, an RMK 20/30x30 and an RMK 50/30x30. Aircraft has retrofitted cowlings with VL-designed carburettor dust filters on both sides of the cowlings. (Kari Stenman coll.)

Bristol Blenheim IV, BL-129, kapt. Aaro Melasniemi, Valok/Lentolaivue 48, Onttola airfield, August 1943.

BL-129 of LeLv 48 between photo missions at Luonetjärvi in summer 1943. The playing card emblem (Ace of Hearts) was bigger in this season. The assigned pilot was the deputy flight leader, kapt. Aaro Melasniemi. (Finnish Air Force Museum)

Bristol Blenheim IV, BL-129, kapt. Aaro Melasniemi, Valok/Lentolaivue 48, Onttola airfield, August 1943.

Ilyushin DB-3M & DB-3F

During the Winter War in 1939–40 a number of DB-3M bombers were captured. Five of them were refurbished and given Finnish serials VP-101, 102 etc. according to the 12 February 1940 order. The first one was serialled VP-101 and while the others were being completed, the serials were amended in December 1940 to VP-11 to VP-15. On 17 September 1941 the serial lettering was changed to DB and and applied to planes 12 and 15.

After the outbreak of the Continuation War six more aircraft were bought from the German war booty depots. These arrived in Finland on 12 September 1941 and they were serialled DB-16 to DB-21. VP-13 came back from Germany, having been sent there on 12 May for evaluation. After repairs it became DB-13. The Finnish Air Force had thus a total of eleven DB-3M aircraft in its inventory.

On 2 October 1942 the Finnish state bought from German war booty depots four examples of DB-3F (Il-4) bombers, which were delivered to the Finns at Bryansk on 13 October for transfer to Finland. The aircraft were serialled DF-22 to DF-25 inclusive. Number 22 was destroyed during the transfer and the remaining three aircraft arrived in Finland on 21 October 1942 and went for overhaul.

DB-3M serial VP-101 of LLv 36 at Helsinki Malmi hangar on 3 March 1940. The aircraft was originally painted overall with aluminium lacquer. This aircraft was earlier "Red 15" and one of five captured in the Winter war and put into Finnish service. (Finnish Air Force)

VP-11 of LLv 46 in spring 1941. The squadron was based at Siikakangas, from where it moved to Luonetjärvi in the Continuation War mobilization. This plane was earlier VP-101, the new serial VP-11 and Warpaint with aluminium lacquer undersides was applied at the air depot in December 1940. (Klaus Niska coll.)

Continuation War

At the outbreak of the war on 25 June 1941 *Lentolaivue* 46 was stationed at Luonetjärvi with *maj.* Niilo Jusu in command. The 1st Flight was equipped with three Blenheim IV bombers and the 2nd Flight had four DB-3M bombers, which were used only for training purposes, until delivered to the new LLv 48.

Lentolaivue 48 was established at Luonetjärvi on 23 November 1941 under *Lentorykmentti* 4. *Maj.* Raoul Harju-Jeanty was appointed in command of the squadron. At first the task was the advanced training for the regiment's needs.

In May 1942 the 2nd Flight was tasked with bombardment and from mid-June 1942 it began to receive from the factory DB-3M bombers. Next month the 1st Flight began to receive Pe-2 dive-bombers. The squadron was to operate around the Maaselkä isthmus, south-west of the White Sea. Not many sorties were flown, as the 2nd Flight had only two bombing missions in 1942.

On 31 August *Lentorykmentti* 4 attacked with 22 aircraft the air base at Segesha. LeLv 48 participated in its first mission and bombed under *kapt.* Siirilä's leadership, with three Dbs, a storage area south of the target. A Russian Tomahawk followed one DB, but lost contact when crossing Lake Seesjärvi.

DB-17 of 2/LeLv 48 revs up at Luonetjärvi in August 1942. Bought from German war booty depots, it was refurbished at the factory, which applied the Warpaint on 20 February 1942. The flight badge is on the nose. (Klaus Niska coll.)

On 17 September the 2/LeLv 48 took off with three DB-3Ms to bomb Nopsa station, along the Murmansk railway. One plane crashed in the forest on take-off. The other two continued and bombed the target, led by *kapt.* Siirilä.

From the beginning of 1943 the 2/LeLv 48 was to carry out regiment bombardments around Olonets. The unit's strength was four serviceable DB-3Ms.

The regiment bombing of Segesha was postponed several times due to poor weather. On 19 February the weather looked more favourable and LeR 4 gave an order to all squadrons to attack the target. After take-off the weather deteriorated quickly when a snowstorm approached from the east. The four DB-3M swarm of *luutn.* Lehto of LeLv 48 was above the target just after 10 pm. Two of the aircraft found the target and dropped their bombs, but in the poor weather could not observe the hits. During the return flight all were disoriented in the snowfall. One aircraft crashed on the ice of Lake Pielinen, another was damaged while landing on frozen Lake Pyhäjärvi, the third bellied at Suomussalmi and the fourth was damaged in a forced landing on the frozen Lake Onkamojärvi. The damaged aircraft were repaired by the end of March.

During the spring the 2/LeLv 48 bombed occasionally the stations and trains on the Murmansk railway with a DB-3M pair, managing to hit a few times a moving train and causing a fire in several wagons.

Before midnight on 20 August LeR 4 concentrated most of its forces to bomb a partisan base at Lehto, west of Belomorsk. The regiment attacked with 31 aircraft and ten Morane fighters flew escort. The 2/LeLv 48 bombed, under *kapt.* Saxell with three DB-3Ms and one DB-3F, the villages. Several houses were damaged and two were set on fire.

In the evening of 17 September the whole regiment carried out the bombardment of Lavansaari air base. LeLv 48 sent to this operation two DB-3Ms lead by *maj.* Kepsu. They bombed the island and returned to the base. On 4 November 1943 the commander of LeR 4 gave an order to transfer the Russian DB-3M and DB-3F bombers from LeLv 48 to the newly established 3rd Flight of LeLv 46. The new arrangements were carried out on 11 November and the task was to attack targets specified by the supreme command.

DB-13 photoplane of LeLv 48 parked at Tiiksjärvi in September 1942. Under the nose hatch was an RMKS/18x24 camera. The Warpaint was applied at the factory in previous April, keeping the aluminium lacquer on lower surfaces. (Pauli Ervi)

LeLv 48 had flown with DB-3Ms 27 sorties and another three by DB-3Fs. Three aircraft were lost in flying accidents with seven of the aircrew killed.

On 1 January 1944 two DB-3Ms and two DB-3Fs were in the inventory of 3/LeLv 46. On 14 February the abbreviation of the squadron was amended to PLeLv 46.

In the evening of 30 March LeR 4 bombed with 33 aircraft Mergino air base south of the mouth of River Svir. PLeLv 46 participated in the attack with five Dorniers and one DB-3M and one DB-3F led by *kapt.* Pesola. Hits were recorded in the target area.

On 3 April the regiment bombed Kähy air base on the Karelian Isthmus, where reconnaissance had discovered over 50 Russian aircraft. *Kapt.* Lehto's four Dorniers, one DB-3M and one DB-3F bombed parked aircraft on the airfield. Several fires were observed after the attack

In the evening of 18 May *Lentorykmentti* 4 again attacked Mergino airfield. Six Dorniers and three DB-3F bombers of PLeLv 46 under *kapt.* Pesola bombed the base. Several fires were lit. The next night the regiment attacked Alehovtshina warehouse complex south of the river Svir. The squadron participated with seven Dorniers, two DB-3Fs and one DB-3M led by *kapt.* Pesola.

In the morning of 9 June the Russians began a major offensive on the Karelian Isthmus in the sector of IV Army Corps, the focus of the assault being between Valkeasaari and the Gulf of Finland. On the same evening LeR 4 was ordered to prepare attacks with all available forces towards the Karelian Isthmus.

DB-17 of 3/PLeLv 46 landing at Luonetjärvi on 31 March 1944. The nose still carried the badge of 2/LeLv 48, where the plane served until 15 November 1943. The lower surfaces received DN-väri *at the factory on 11 February 1943. (SA-kuva)*

Out of the 25 full regiment attacks during the next two months, 3/PLeLv 46 participated in 15, usually with 2–4 Ilyushin bombers, attacking enemy troops, tanks, artillery and shipping on the Karelian Isthmus, Gulf of Viipuri and north of Lake Ladoga.

On 9 August the 3/PLeLv 46 flew its last mission in the Continuation War by bombing with *kapt.* Lehto's four aircraft (1DN, 2 DB and 1 DF) the station at Suojärvi.

On 4 September 1944 the hostilities against the Soviet Union came to an end by a cease-fire.

PLeLv 46 had flown 44 sorties with DB-3Ms and another 28 with DB-3Fs. No aircraft were lost on operations. One DB-3M and one DB-3F were destroyed in flying accidents. Three aircrew lost their lives.

Lapland War

According to the terms of the truce, the German forces had to be removed from Finland by 15 September 1944. When the Germans had not retreated from Lapland by the deadline, the Finns began its offensive to the north.

S/n	Delivered	Struck off charge	Remarks	Flying Hours
VP-101, VP-11	29 Feb 1940	20 May 1942	W/o Hirvaslampi 30 June1941	82.15
VP-12, DB-12	27 Jun 1941	13 Nov 1942	W/o Luonetjärvi 19 Aug 1942	62.55
VP-13, DB-13	21 Feb 1941	10 Jan 1946	Last flight 1 Nov 1945	372.50
VP-14	14 Mar 1941	17 Jul 1941	W/o Konnevesi 2 Jul 1941	26.05
VP-15, DB-15	24 Jun 1941	17 Jun 1943	W/o Pielinen 19 Feb 1943	231.05
DB-16	12 Sep 1941	29 Dec 1944	W/o Ounasjoki 22 Oct 1944	270.35
DB-17	12 Sep 1941	31 May 1946	Last flight 26 Sep 1945	418.10
DB-18	12 Sep 1941	15 Dec 1942	W/o Höytiäinen 17 Sep 1942	72.35
DB-19	12 Sep 1941	9 Jan 1946	Last flight 28 Feb 1945	225.50
DB-20	12 Sep 1941	30 Aug 1944	W/o Mensuvaara 29 Feb 1944	106.50
DB-21	12 Sep 1941	9 Jan 1946	W/o Tampere 4 Oct 1945	238.50
DF-22		31 Dec 1942	W/o Roslawl 14 Oct 1942	
DF-23	2 Nov 1942	29 Sep 1945	W/o Tampere 23 Feb 1945	169.50
DF-24	2 Nov 1942	20 Mar 1945	W/o Mensuvaara 16 Jun 1944	51.05
DF-25	2 Nov 1942	29 Sep 1945	W/o Öija 3 Jan 1945	103.35

Special Detachment Sarko was formed for Lapland air operations and *Lentorykmentti* 2 and 4 were subordinated to it. Bombing squadrons 42, 44, 46 and 48 belonged to *Lentorykmentti* 4. PLeLv 46 had three Dorniers, three DB-3Ms and two DB-3Fs.

PLeLv 46 went in action in the Lapland War on 2 October, attacking German troops and vehicles on the road from Kemi to Rovaniemi. *Luutn*. Lampelto's detachment had two Dorniers, two DB-3Ms and one DB-3F.

The last mission of the Ilyushin bombers was flown on 22 March 1945, when a German barracks area north of Lake Kilpisjärvi was attacked with one Dornier and one DB-3M.

In the Lapland War the DB-3Ms flew 21 sorties and the DB-3Fs another nine. German flak shot down one DB-3M, and one DB-3F was lost in an accident. There were no personnel losses.

During 1945 two DB-3M and one DB-3F bombers were damaged in flying accidents. The last flight was performed on 1 November 1945 and the aircraft were put into storage and scrapped two months later.

DF-25 of 3/PLeLv 46 warming up at Luonetjärvi on 31 March 1944. This particular machine was fitted with M-88B engines. The regulation Warpaint was done at the factory on 16 June 1943. The DN-väri underside shows here beautifully. (SA-kuva)

Ilyushin DB-3M & DB-3F
Camouflage and markings

The first DB-3M, which was captured on 29 January 1940 in fully airworthy condition, retained its aluminium lacquer overall finish. The Soviet markings were painted over and the Finnish national insignias and serial number VP-101 applied instead.

The serial number was changed to VP-11 in December 1940 and in this connection the aircraft received the new Warpaint introduced on 30 September 1940: Olive Green and Black upper sides, lower sides remaining in aluminium lacquer.

On 17 September 1941 the rather confusing serial numbering of captured bombers was solved by giving separate type identifications, for the DB-3M this was DB with the consecutive numbers being the same, DB-12, 15 and 18–21.

The other four war booty DB-3Ms received a similar Warpaint in a major repair and overhaul at the State Aircraft factory, with serials VP-12 to VP-15. The first three of the six DB-3M aircraft, which were bought from the German war booty stocks, were painted in the same way.

The second three plane lot was completed after the introduction of the *DN-väri* lower sides on 7 May 1942 and was painted accordingly with this. Also the upper surfaces retained the same Olive Green and Black colours, but the pattern was the new splinter type issued to captured aircraft.

All three DB-3F aircraft received the splinter pattern Warpaint with *DN-väri* undersides in the factory repair.

Of the older aircraft DB-12 was the first to get the *DN-väri* undersides on 1 August 1942. DB-17 followed on 11 February 1943 and DB-13 and – 16 in February 1944.

These colours remained on the aircraft until November 1945, when the last one was put into storage and later scrapped.

VP-101 of LLv 46 on a visit to Joroinen in summer 1940. The serial was amended to VP-11 in December. The overall colour is aluminium lacquer. The wing insignia are according to contemporary regulations, 4/5th of the chord. Behind is a row of LLv 26 FIAT's. (Carl-Erik Bruun)

DB-20 of 2/LeLv 48 at Luonetjärvi in June 1943. The splinter pattern of the Warpaint is clearly seen. Wing insignias are according to the 100 cm regulation dated 23 July 1940. (Lauri Onnela)

DF-25 of 3/PLeLv 46 during an overhaul at Luonetjärvi. On 9 April 1944 kers. Paavo Karpiola flew the plane back to its base at Mensuvaara. (SA-kuva)

Ilyushin DB-3M, VP-101, Lentolaivue 36, Helsinki Malmi airfield, March 1940. Overall aluminium dope. Serial Black.

VP-101 belonging now to LLv 46, as seen at Luonetjärvi on 6 April 1940. The serial was changed to VP-11 in December 1940. The overall aluminium lacquer finish still looks pristine. (Finnish Air Force)

Ilyushin DB-3M, VP-11, 2/Lentolaivue 46, Luonetjärvi airfield, June 1941. Camouflage colours: upper surfaces Olive Green and Black, under surfaces aluminium dope. Standard Eastern Front markings Yellow, serial Black and Olive Green.

VP-11 of 2/LLv 46 seen at Luonetjärvi in the second half of June 1941. The aircraft was destroyed on 30 June 1941, when an engine failed, causing the aircraft to crash in Lake Hirvaslampi. (Lassi Eskola)

91

Ilyushin DB-3M, DB-13, 2/Lentolaivue 48, Luonetjärvi airfield, July 1942. Camouflage colours: upper surfaces Olive Green and Black, under surfaces aluminium dope. Standard Eastern Front markings brighter Lemon Yellow, serial Black and Olive Green.

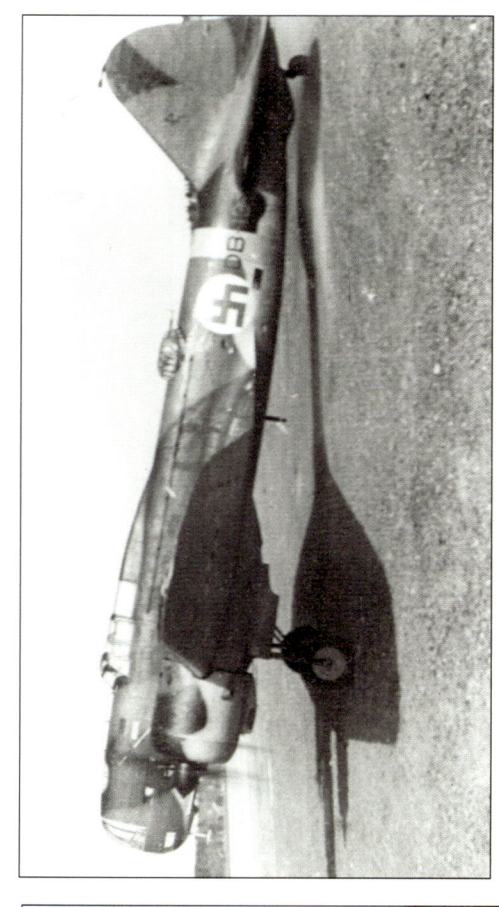

DB-13 of Photoflight Ahtiainen seen at Luonetjärvi in summer 1942. The regulation Warpaint with aluminium lacquer underside was applied in previous April. The farting elk emblem of 2/LeLv 24 was added on the fin of the aircraft during a visit to Tiiksjärvi. (Kari Stenman coll.)

DB-13 of Photoflight Ahtiainen of LeLv 48 at Luonetjärvi in summer 1942. The regular pilot was vänr. Aarne Vatanen. The yellow eastern front markings were quite possibly in the brighter lemon Yellow. (Lassi Eskola)

Ilyushin DB-3M, DB-18, 2/Lentolaivue 48, Luonetjärvi airfield, August 1942. Camouflage colours: upper surfaces Olive Green and Black, under surfaces aluminium dope. Standard Eastern Front markings Yellow, serial Black and Olive Green.

DB-18 of 2/LeLv 48 at Luonetjärvi in August 1942. The bear emblem on the bomber's nose is the flight badge. The regular pilot was luutn. Alpo Lehto, though mostly training flights were performed. (Finnish Air Force)

Ilyushin DB-3M, DB-18, 2/Lentolaivue 48, Luonetjärvi airfield, August 1942.

Above: DB-18 of 2/LeLv 48 parked at Luonetjärvi in summer 1942. Combat missions were rare as the DB-3s flew only five sorties in 1942. (Kari Stenman coll.) Right: The line-up of 2/LeLv 48 at Luonetjärvi in summer 1942. Aircraft are DB-15 (nearest), 18, 17 and 19. (Lassi Eskola)

94

*Ilyushin DB-3M, DB-18, 2/Lentolaivue 48,
Luonetjärvi airfield, August 1942.*

DB-19 of 2/LeLv 48 at Luonetjärvi in August 1942. The regular pilot was the flight leader kapt. Yrjö Siirilä. The in-flight view reveals the splinter pattern of the Warpaint as applied to captured aircraft, as applied from 7 May 1942 onwards. (Finnish Air Force)

Ilyushin DB-3M, DB-19, 2/Lentolaivue 48, Luonetjärvi airfield, August 1942.

97

Ilyushin DB-3F (Il-4), DF-23, 2/Lentolaivue 48, Luonetjärvi airfield, August 1943. Camouflage colours: upper surfaces Olive Green and Black, under surfaces DN-väri. Standard Eastern Front markings Yellow, serial Black and Olive Green.

Fully repaired and overhauled DF-23 at the air depot located at Tampere on 5 June 1943, when the aircraft was delivered to LeLv 48. The engines are M-88Bs, but with the older DB-3M style cowlings. (Finnish Air Force)

Ilyushin DB-3F (Il-4), DF-23, 2/Lentolaivue 48, Luonetjärvi airfield, August 1943.

DF-23 of 2/LeLv 48 at Luonetjärvi in summer 1943. The Warpaint with DN-väri undersides was applied at the State Aircraft Factory on 15 April 1943. All other markings are regulation items as well. (Lauri Onnela)

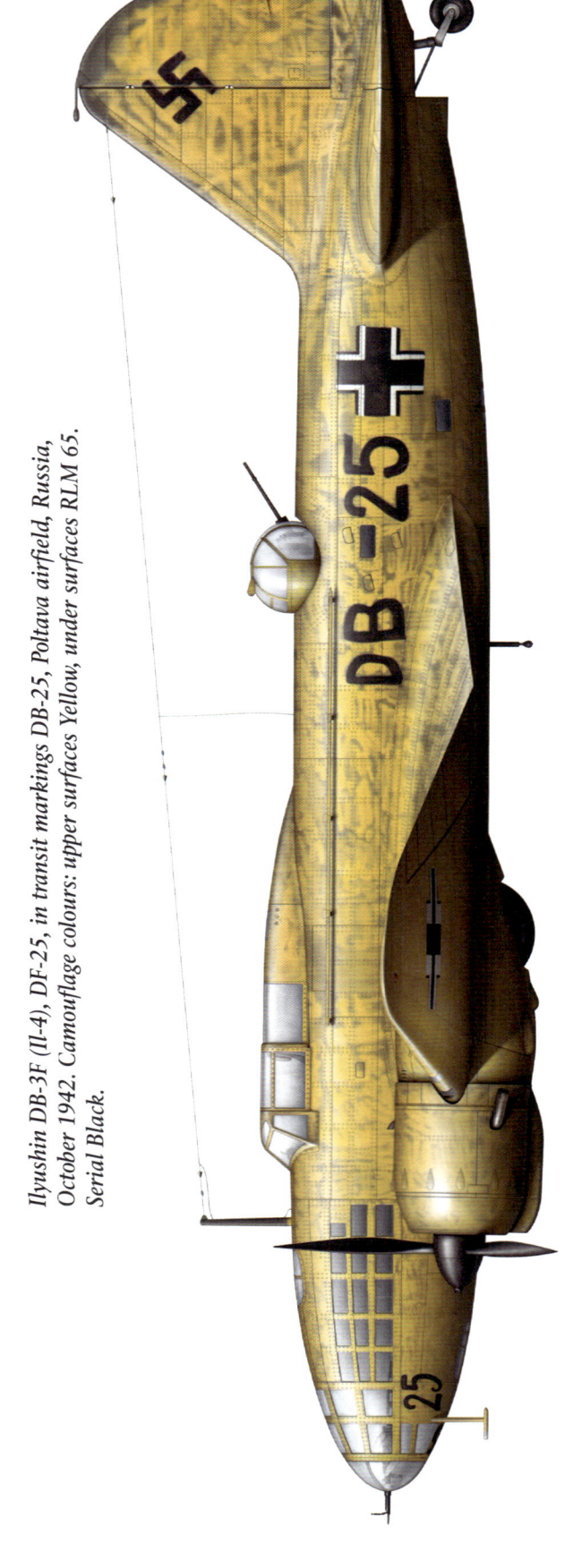

Ilyushin DB-3F (Il-4), DF-25, in transit markings DB-25, Poltava airfield, Russia, October 1942. Camouflage colours: upper surfaces Yellow, under surfaces RLM 65. Serial Black.

Ilyushin DB-3F, incorrectly serialled as DB-25 after hand-over to Finnish aircrews at Poltava on 13 October 1942. The aircraft arrived in Finland a week later. The upper surfaces have been covered with a patchy and uneven Yellow paint, common to German war booty planes. (Lassi Eskola)

Ilyushin DB-3F (Il-4), DF-25, 3/Pommituslentolaivue 46, Luonetjärvi airfield, March 1944. Camouflage colours: upper surfaces Olive Green and Black, under surfaces DN-väri. Standard Eastern Front markings Yellow; serial Black and Olive Green.

DF-25 of 3/PLeLv 46 photographed during an overhaul at Luonetjärvi on 31 March 1944. The regular pilot was vänr. Erkki Bohm. All markings are strictly to the regulations. (SA-kuva)

Douglas DC-2

Swedish Count Carl Gustav von Rosen donated one DC-2 to the Finnish Air Force and flew it to Finland in mid-January 1940. It received the serial DC-1 and nickname Hanssin-Jukka. The overall colour was a Swedish Air Force lower surface Light Bluegrey. The serial was changed to the final DO-1 on 12 March 1942.

The aircraft was delivered to LLv 44 on 19 February 1940 and flew one bombing mission during the Winter War, on 1 March 1940. On 25 April the plane was handed over to LLv 46 for transport duties.

At the beginning of the Continuation War it flew supply and ambulance missions for the advancing Finnish troops. On 29 November 1941 it was transferred to LLv 28 for cartography missions.

On 1 March 1942 Hanssin-Jukka was sent to the air depot, which applied Warpaint on 9 March. Then it was delivered to the Air Force Headquarters, where is was used as a personnel transport on international flights for six months.

On 11 November 1942 it received new Warpaint with *DN-väri* undersides during a major overhaul at the depot. On 8 March 1943 the HQ resumed the international flights, which ended in a landing accident at Insterburg, Germany on 20 June 1944.

Douglas DC-2 airliner serialled DC-1 of 2/LLv 44 as a bomber seen at Joroinen. On 1 March 1940 it flew the sole bombing mission in the Winter War, piloted by the donator Erik von Rosen, who held then the rank of luutnantti. *Note the nose and dorsal guns and the bomb racks. (Finnish Aviation Museum)*

DC-1 of LLv 46 photographed at Luonetjärvi on 2 August 1940. The aircraft came from Sweden and it is assumed that the overall colour was the Swedish Air Force lower surface Light Bluegrey. The serial is also under both wing tips. Inscription on the nose is HANSSIN-JUKKA. (Finnish Air Force)

Lufthansa repaired the plane and handed over it to LeR 4 in early August 1944 for supply missions in the Lapland War. After the war LeR 4 operated the plane until 1 June 1955, when it had logged 7579.35 hours. The airframe was placed at Hämeenlinna as a cafeteria until 1981. The aircraft was then restored and is now on exhibit at the Finnish Air Force Museum.

DC-1 of LLv 46 between supply missions at Lunkula dry beach of Lake Ladoga on 8 September 1941. It carried fuel to advancing Finnish tanks and brought back wounded soldiers. Yellow eastern front markings were added during the mobilization a couple of months earlier. (Esko Rinne)

Douglas DC-2
Camouflage and markings

Before being flown to Finland in January 1940 the aircraft was painted in Sweden to a uniform Light Bluegrey. finish, almost certainly with the Swedish Air Force underside colour *Ljust Blå-grå*. This colour was still worn when the yellow Eastern Front markings were applied in June 1941. The serial DC-1 was also painted under the wings.

On 1 March 1942 the aircraft was sent to the State Aircraft factory for Warpaint application. This Black and Olive Green camouflage was done eight days later. Also the serial was changed to DO-1 in this connection.

In September 1942 the aircraft was sent to the factory for an engine change, from Cyclones to the M-62s. Here the plane received a new Warpaint on 11 November 1942, with Light Blue-Grey *DN-väri* undersides. A year later DO-1 got a new and similar third Warpaint This camouflage remained on the plane until its removal in June 1949.

DO-1 of IlmavE took pilots to Germany to pick up Messerschmitts in March 1943. The serial DC-1 was changed on 12 March 1942 to DO-1. In this connection it also received the first Warpaint. The camouflage in the photo was the second Warpaint done at the depot on 11 November 1942 with DN-väri undersides. (Pauli Ervi)

Douglas DC-2, DC-1, Lentolaivue 46, Lunkula landing ground, September 1941. Camouflage colours: overall Light Bluegrey. Standard Eastern Front markings Yellow, serial Black.

HANSSIN-JUKKA

DC-1 of LLv 46 on the dry beach at Lunkula in September 1941. The overall colour is thought to be Swedish Air Forced underside Light Bluegrey, as this aircraft came as a donation from Sweden. (Finnish Air Force Museum)

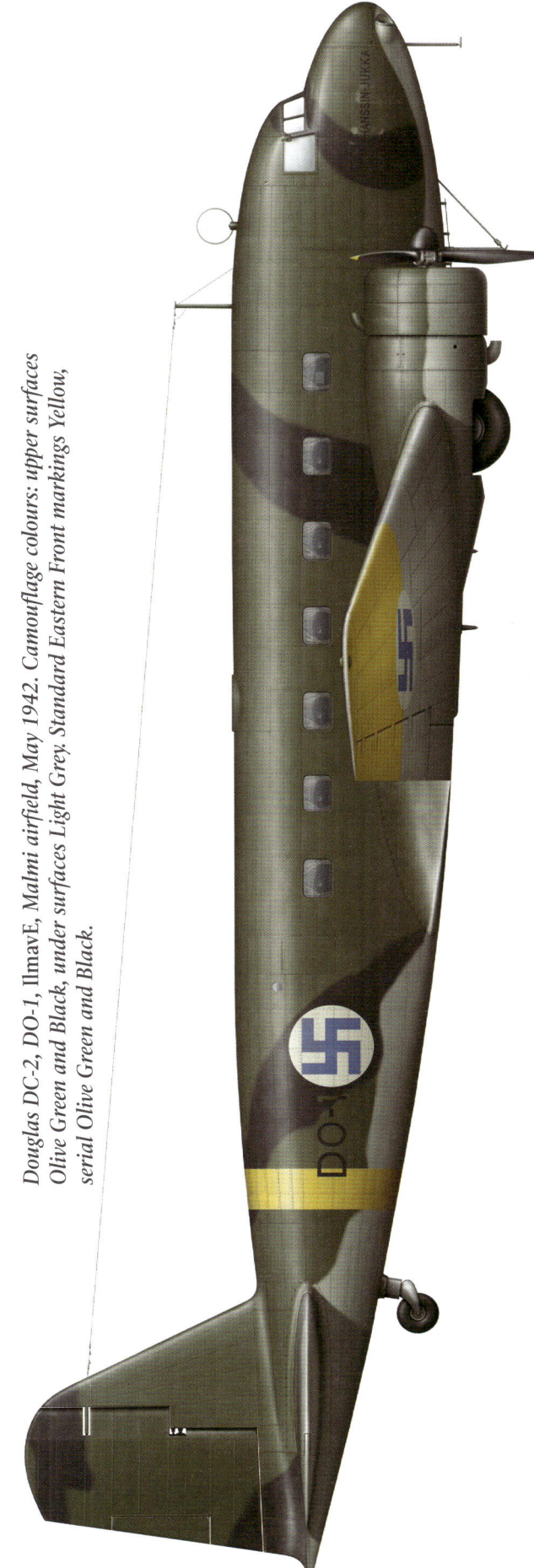

Douglas DC-2, DO-1, IlmavE, Malmi airfield, May 1942. Camouflage colours: upper surfaces Olive Green and Black, under surfaces Light Grey. Standard Eastern Front markings Yellow, serial Olive Green and Black.

DO-1 in its first Warpaint, which was specially applied on 9 March 1942 at the air depot, where the photo was taken. The regulation underside colour was then aluminium lacquer for metal covered aircraft, but here it seems to be the other generally used colour, Light Grey. (Finnish Air Force Museum)

Douglas DC-2, DO-1, IlmaVE, Malmi airfield, May 1943. Camouflage colours: upper surfaces Olive Green and Black, under surfaces DN-väri. Standard Eastern Front markings Yellow, serial Black.

DO-1 of IlmavE as a VIP transport during its career, seen here at Helsinki Malmi in spring 1943. The Warpaint is the second one, done by the depot on 11 November 1942. (Kari Stenman coll.)

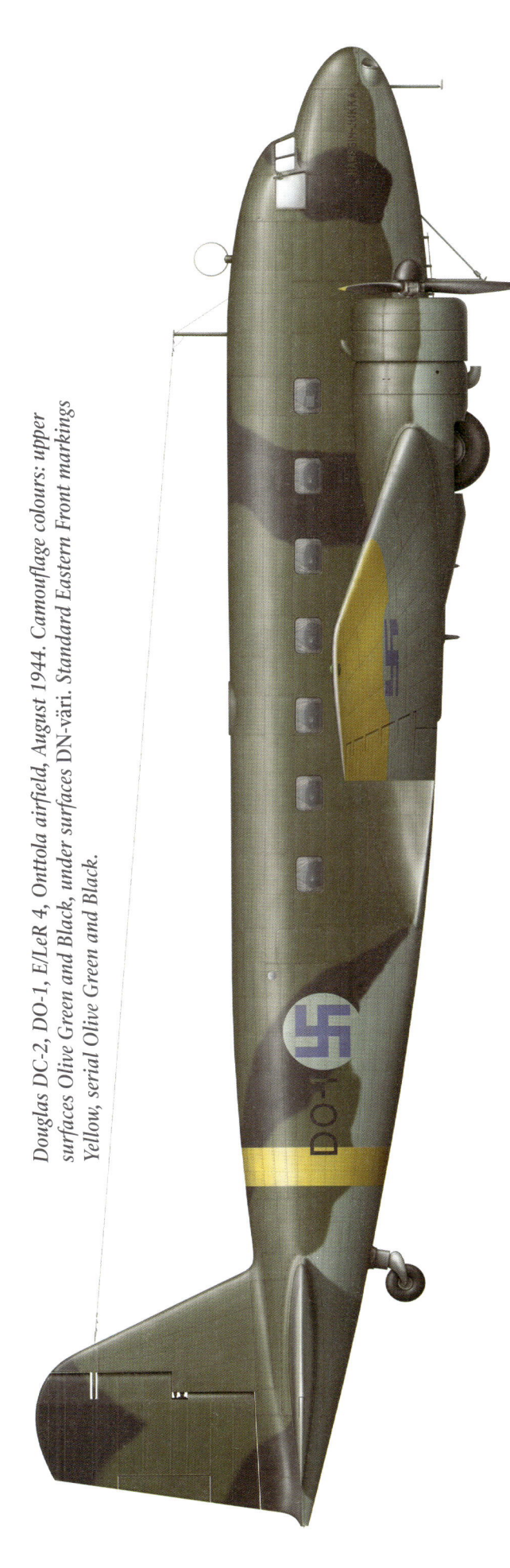

Douglas DC-2, DO-1, E/LeR 4, Onttola airfield, August 1944. Camouflage colours: upper surfaces Olive Green and Black, under surfaces DN-väri. Standard Eastern Front markings Yellow, serial Olive Green and Black.

DO-1 still named HANSSIN-JUKKA of LeR 4 in its third Warpaint, which was done at the factory in December 1943. The left photo shows the plane at Kemi in October 1944 and the right photo exposes the nose from the other side. (Kari Stenman coll.)

Westland Lysander I

The Westland Lysander I was one of the types which the British government approved for sale to Finland after the beginning of the Winter War. On 8 January 1940 an order was placed for 17 aircraft. The first nine were shipped to Finland and the remaining eight were planned to be ferried by air.

The air route was much faster, but only two aircraft (serials LY-123 and 125) arrived on 8 March 1940, one (LY-124) being lost in transit in Stavanger, Norway. The shipped batch arrived in Gothenburg, Sweden for assembly and after that were flown to Finland, the first three arriving on 21 March 1940, the next two on 24 March, followed by two on 4 April and the last one arriving on 3 May 1940. The serials for these were LY-114 to LY-122 inclusive. The Finnish Air Force had a total of twelve Lysanders.

Lysander LY-123 of LLv 12 at Utti in mid-July 1940. The aircraft carries the standard British army co-op scheme of Dark Green and Dark Earth upper sides with aluminium lacquer lower sides of the flying surfaces. Serial font is British style. National insignia are by the 4/5th of the chord. (Finnish Air Force)

LY-125 of 2/LLv 16 at Höytiäinen beach near Joensuu in the second half of July 1941. The regular pilot was the flight leader luutn. Veikko Härmälä. The aircraft was repaired at the factory in July 1940, applying the Finnish font serial, smaller fuselage insignia and some paintwork. (Finnish Air Force)

Continuation War

By the start of the new conflict the Lysanders were all issued to the 2nd Flight of LLv 16, subjected for Karelian Army and tasked with reconnaissance, tactical photography, harassment bombing and army co-operation missions. On 25 June 1941 the flight possessed three Lysanders and shortly received the fourth, which was to be the biggest number available at any one time.

On 5 August at 5.10 am seven I-153s escorted by three MiG-3s strafed Värtsilä base and set fire to two LLv 16 Lysanders, damaging a third, leaving only one Lysander operational.

On 3 September 1941 three I-16 fighters took by surprise a Lysander of 2/LLv 16 on a message delivery mission to Kivatsu station, commencing at 11.55 am. The crew of LY-121 was *ylikers.* Eero Pakarinen as pilot and *korpr.* Reino Pesu as gunner. After repeated attacks one I-16 managed to score hits causing the pilot to crash land his Lysander into the forest, but not before the gunner had made lethal hits on the enemy fighter.

At the beginning of 1942 there were two airworthy Lysanders in 2/LLv 16. The occasional reconnaissance missions were carried out by single planes throughout the year. When 1943 started *Lentolaivue* 16 had three serviceable Lysanders. Missions were still carried out by single planes until the summer.

LY-121 of 2/LLv 16 at Värtsilä in August 1941. The finish is the original British one from the late 1930s. When piloted by ylikers. Eero Pakarinen, this aircraft was forced to crash by three I-16 fighters on 3 September 1941, but not before the rear gunner korpr. Reino Pesu had managed to down one of them. (Finnish Aviation Museum)

LY-120 of 2/LLv 16 at Värtsilä, where it arrived on 23 September 1941. It was regularly flown by luutn. Tom Simberg. The Warpaint was applied at the factory one week earlier, with aluminium lacquer lower surfaces. (Kari Stenman coll.)

On 19 May the 2nd and 3rd Flights of LeLv 16 flew a joint operation by bombing a fuel storage nearby Juka station. Just before midnight five Fokker C.Xs and three Lysanders dropped from 900 metres a total 2225 kg of bombs and incendiaries. Two explosions occurred in the storage area creating high and strong flames. Juka station received 120 kg incendiaries, lighting one fire.

On 22 June LeLv 16 flew another squadron bombing by attacking an ammunition storage north-east of Haapaselkä. At 21.40 hours four C.Xs and three Lysanders dropped from 900 metres 2005 kg bombs and incendiaries, hitting the target area, where one strong explosion was observed.

On 27 July LeLv 16 performed the last joint bombing mission by attacking a base at the Voivanets river in the Maaselkä Isthmus. At 21.40 four C.Xs and two Lysanders dropped 1825 kg bombs and incendiaries from 900 metres. Two small fires were lit.

The damage inflicted with these joint attacks was not considered worthwhile. Also the few planes were at risked from flak. From now on the Lysanders were employed in low-risk reconnaissance missions by single planes, until the last sortie of TLeLv 16, which was performed on 8 August 1944.

By this TLeLv 16 had lost six Lysanders, four on operations, killing two airmen.

On 16 June 1944 TLeLv 16 handed over two Lysanders to TLeLv 14, which operated the type until the cease-fire on 4 September 1944. The last flight of the type was made on 22 November 1945.

A silver-colour Diana painted on the fin was the emblem of 2/LeLv 16 Lysanders. Here LY-120 is paying a visit to Nurmoila on 8 June 1942. The pilot on this occasion was kers. Jalo Laakso. The bomb racks on the wheel spats have been removed as almost useless. (Aulis Bremer)

S/n	Delivered	Struck off charge	Remarks	Flying Hours
LY-114	21 Mar 1940	17 Jul 1941	W/o Lake Ladoga 30 Jun 1941	105.25
LY-115	24 Mar 1940	2 Mar 1946	Last flight 22 Nov 1945	463.05
LY-116	4 Apr 1940	2 Jan 1950	W/o Oulu 8 Dec 1944	330.20
LY-117	21 Mar 1940	30 Aug 1941	W/o 5 Värtsilä Aug 1941	98.35
LY-118	21 Mar 1940	10 Oct 1942	W/o Hirvas 9 Aug 1942	130.20
LY-119	3 May 1940	2 Jan 1950	Into storage 30 Aug 1944	332.20
LY-120	21 Mar 1940	9 Aug 1944	W/o Onttola 4 Jul 1944	326.15
LY-121	4 Apr 1940	31 Dec 1941	W/o Tsalkki 3 Sep 1941	206.55
LY-122	21 Mar 1940	23 Aug 1941	W/o Taipalsaari 30 May 1941	98.15
LY-123	8 Mar 1940	23 Aug 1941	W/o Taipalsaari 9 Jun 1941	103.15
LY-124		26 Jul 1940	W/o Stavanger 2 Mar 1940	
LY-125	8 Mar 1940	30 Aug 1941	W/o Värtsilä 5 Aug 1941	239.20

2/LLv 16 airmen prepare for a mission with LY-119 at Viiksjärvi on 17 February 1942. Unusually this machine has a yellow nose, normally seen only on fighters. The fuselage and wing top insignias have reduced white areas, common to low-flying reconnaissance aircraft. From left are kers. Oiva Kosonen, the flight leader luutn. Veikko Härmälä giving the final briefing and luutn. Göran Kullberg. (SA-kuva)

Westland Lysander I
Camouflage and markings

On arrival in spring 1940 the Lysanders wore the standard RAF colours: Dark Green and Dark Earth upper sides and fuselage with aluminium lacquer undersides to the flying surfaces.

After the introduction of Warpaint (Olive Green and Black upper surfaces) on 30 September 1940, the first Lysander to received this was LY-119 on 25 June 1941, followed by LY-120 on 15 September 1941 and LY-118 on 11 February 1942. The lower surfaces retained their aluminium lacquer finish.

When orders to paint the underside *DN-väri* came on 7 May 1942, this was applied, together with new Warpaint, on LY-116 first on 30 June 1942. LY-119 on 12 September followed by LY-115 on 11 November 1942 and finally LY-120 on 18 January 1943. These colours remained until the end of their flying careers.

During the winters of 1942/43 and 1943/44 all serviceable Lysanders had white winter wash applied, which was usually removed during March.

LY-121 of LLv 30 running up at Pori shortly before the Continuation War, as evidenced by the lack of yellow theatre markings, which were applied on 18 June 1941. The service with LLv 30 ended next month, when the aircraft was delivered to the type's regular user LLv 16. (Reino Lampelto)

Westland Lysander Mk I, LY-121, 2/Lentolaivue 16, Värtsilä airfield, August 1941. Camouflage colours: upper surfaces Dark Green and Dark Earth, underside of flying surfaces aluminium dope. Standard Eastern Front markings Yellow, serial British style Black.

LY-121 of 2/LLv 16 at Värtsilä in August 1941, with the Yellow eastern front markings, but still in the British camouflage. For most of the Continuation War the Lysanders were used in harassment bombings, in addition to the routine reconnaissance duties. (Finnish Aviation Museum)

113

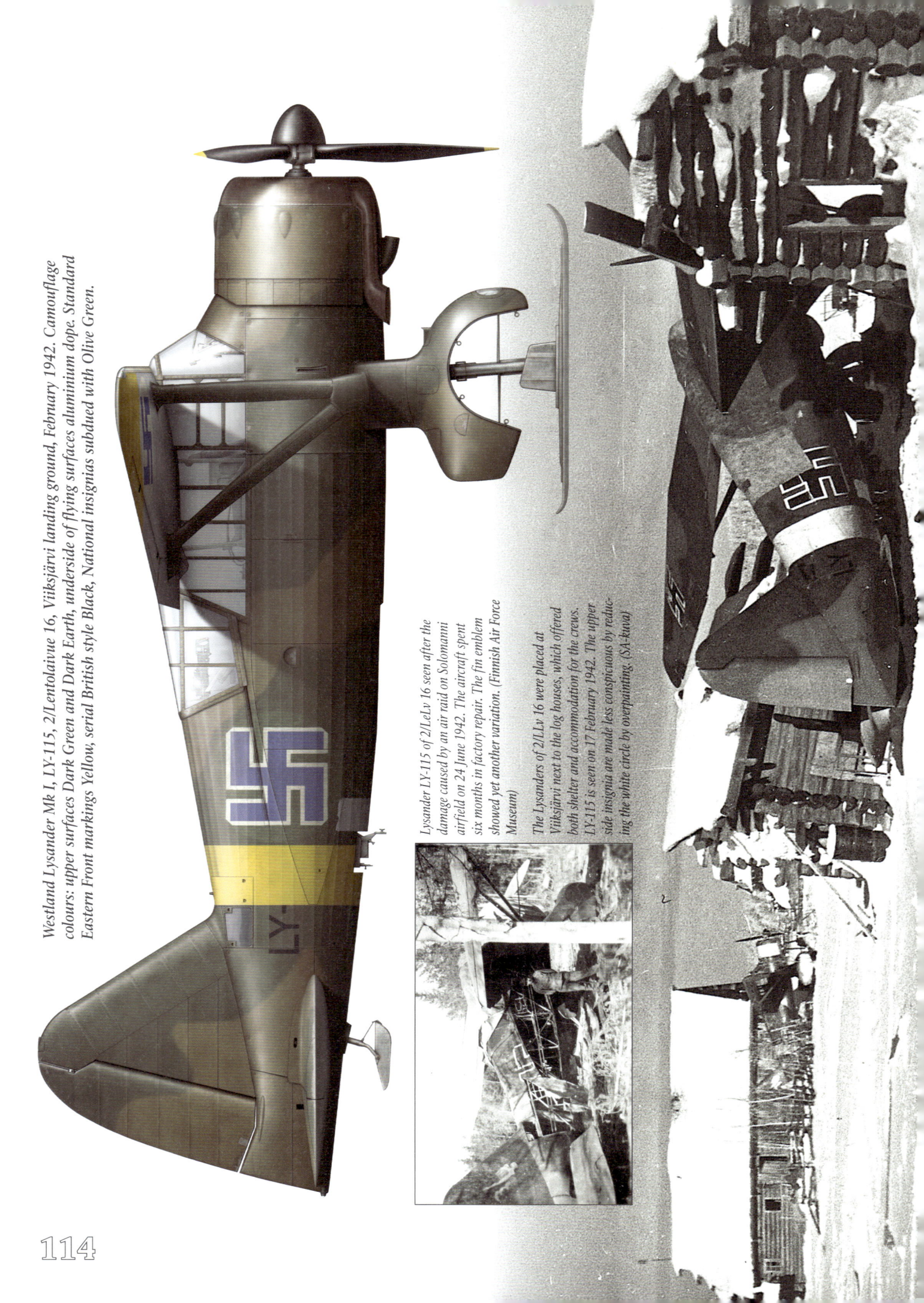

Westland Lysander Mk I, LY-115, 2/Lentolaivue 16, Viiksjärvi landing ground, February 1942. Camouflage colours: upper surfaces Dark Green and Dark Earth, underside of flying surfaces aluminium dope. Standard Eastern Front markings Yellow, serial British style Black, National insignias subdued with Olive Green.

Lysander LY-115 of 2/LeLv 16 seen after the damage caused by an air raid on Solomanni airfield on 24 June 1942. The aircraft spent six months in factory repair. The fin emblem showed yet another variation. (Finnish Air Force Museum)

The Lysanders of 2/LLv 16 were placed at Viiksjärvi next to the log houses, which offered both shelter and accommodation for the crews. LY-115 is seen on 17 February 1942. The upper side insignia are made less conspicuous by reducing the white circle by overpainting. (SA-kuva)

114

Westland Lysander Mk I, LY-115, 2/Lentolaivue 16, Viiksijärvi landing ground, February 1942.

Westland Lysander Mk I, LY-119, 2/Lentolaivue 16, Viiksjärvi landing ground, February 1942. Camouflage colours: upper surfaces Olive Green and Black, under surfaces aluminium dope. Standard Eastern Front markings Yellow, serial Black. National insignias subdued with Olive Green.

Lysander LY-119 of 2/LLv 16 ready for a mission at Viiksjärvi, next to the log house, on 17 February 1942. The Warpaint with aluminium lacquer underside was applied at the factory on 25 June 1941. The detail photo shows the painting of the flight emblem, Diana, on the tail of LY-119. (SA-kuva)

Westland Lysander Mk I, LY-119, 2/Lentolaivue 16, Hirvas airfield, September 1943. Camouflage colours: upper surfaces Olive Green and Black, under surfaces DN-väri. Standard Eastern Front markings Yellow, serial Olive Green and Black.

LY-119 of 2/LeLv 16 at Hirvas during autumn 1943. The paintwork was touched up at the depot on 20 April, keeping the DN-väri undersides and covering the flight badge. (Pentti Manninen coll.)

Westland Lysander Mk I, LY-118, 2/Lentolaivue 16, Hirvas airfield, August 1942. Camouflage colours: upper surfaces Olive Green and Black, under surfaces aluminium dope. Standard Eastern Front markings Yellow, serial Olive Green and Black.

LY-118 of 2/LeLv 16 paying a visit to Tiiksjärvi on 5 August 1942. The pilot on this occasion was kers. Uolevi Paavolainen. This plane crashed at take-off only four days later. The Warpaint was done at the factory on 11 February 1942, with aluminium lacquer lower surfaces. (Pauli Ervi)

Westland Lysander Mk I, LY-118, 2/Lentolaivue 16, Hirvas airfield, August 1942.

119

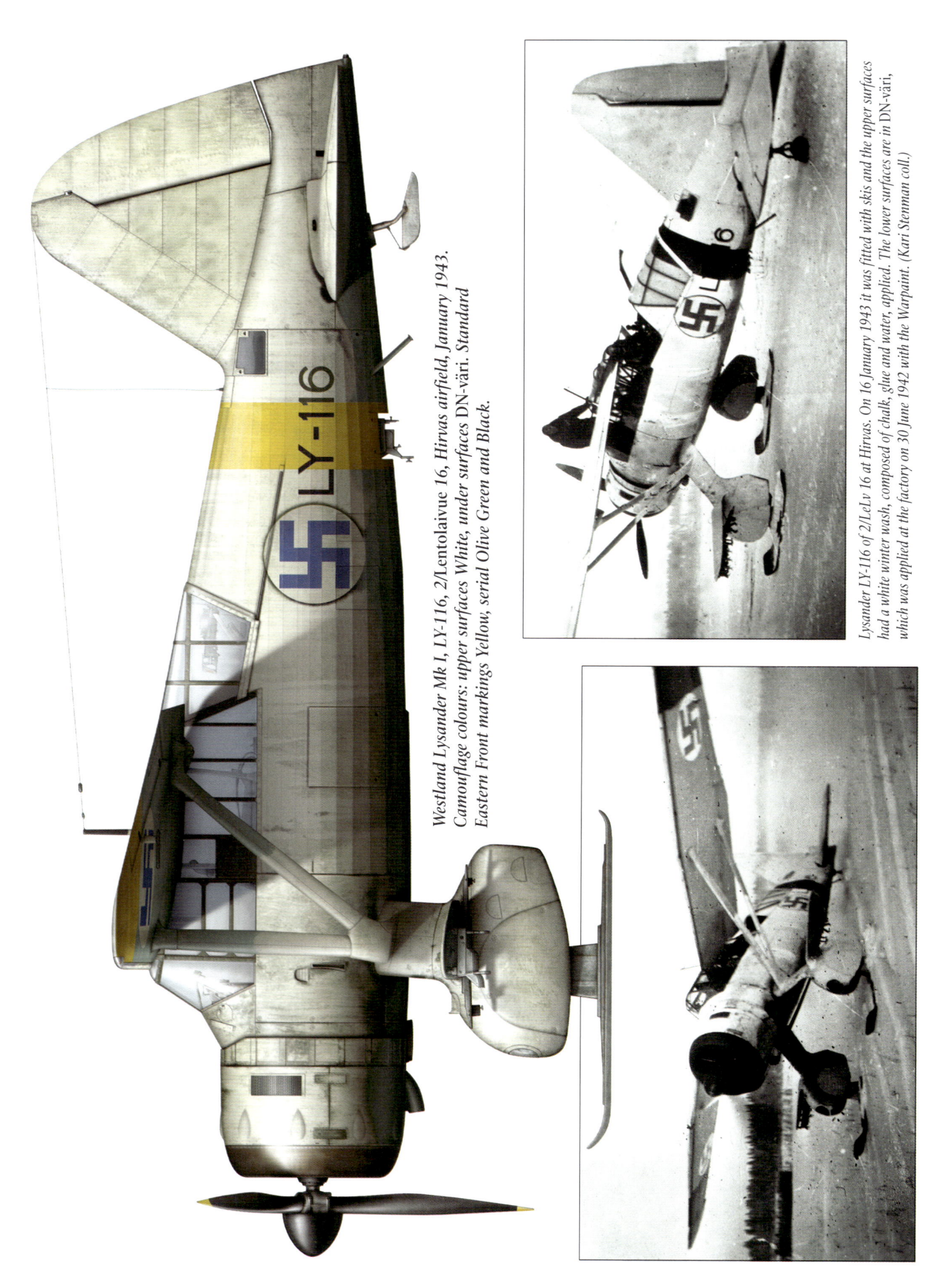

Westland Lysander Mk I, LY-116, 2/Lentolaivue 16, Hirvas airfield, January 1943. Camouflage colours: upper surfaces White, under surfaces DN-väri. Standard Eastern Front markings Yellow, serial Olive Green and Black.

Lysander LY-116 of 2/LeLv 16 at Hirvas. On 16 January 1943 it was fitted with skis and the upper surfaces had a white winter wash, composed of chalk, glue and water, applied. The lower surfaces are in DN-väri, which was applied at the factory on 30 June 1942 with the Warpaint. (Kari Stenman coll.)

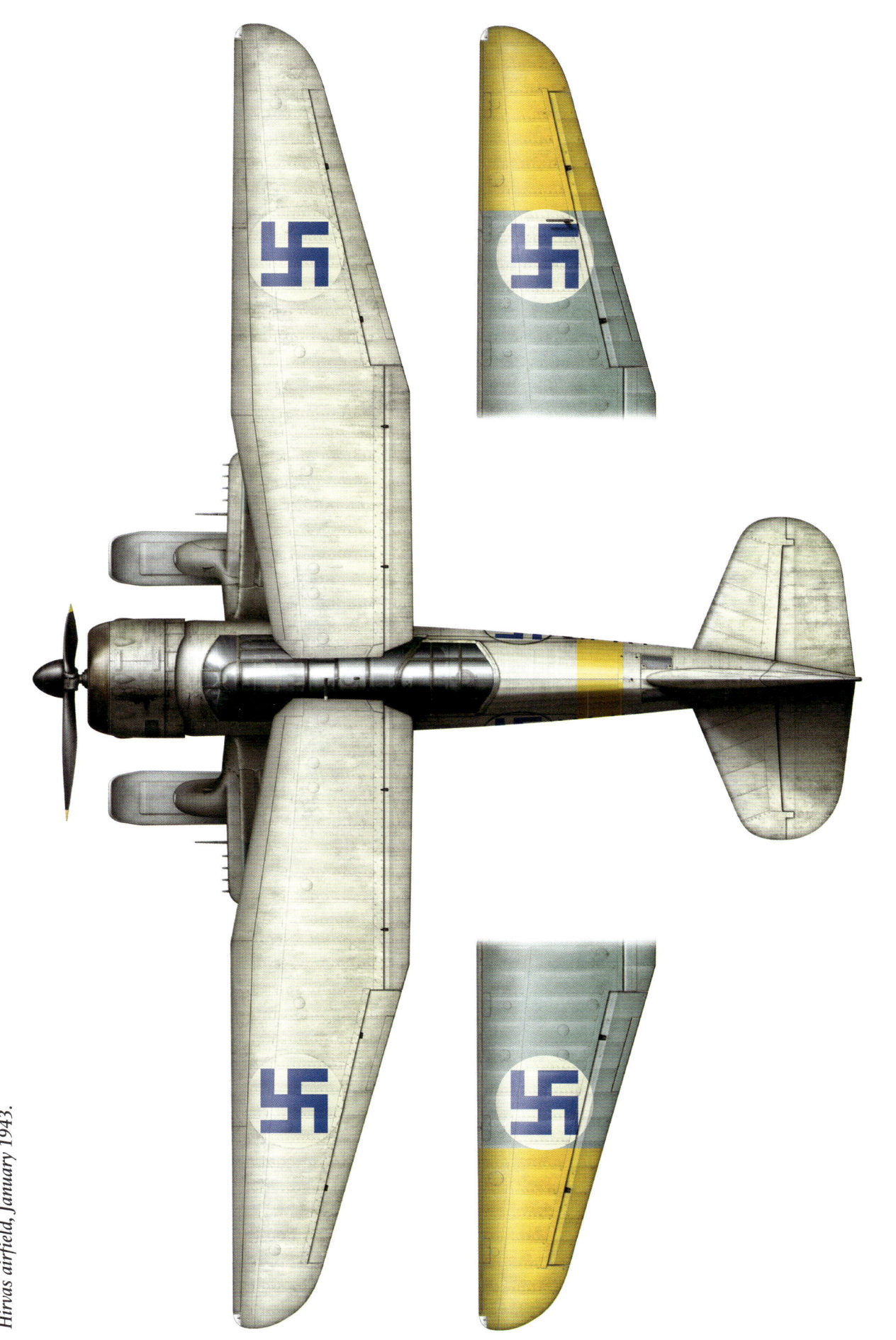

Westland Lysander Mk I, LY-116, 2/Lentolaivue 16, Hirvas airfield, January 1943.

Tupolev SB

Out of the aircraft captured after forced landings during the Winter War in 1939–40, the Finns refurbished eight SB bombers, which according a to 12 February 1940 order were to be serialled VP-10, – 11 etc. The first one repaired was given the serial VP-10 and in December 1940 the serial numbers were changed to VP-1, VP-2 etc. The remaining seven became VP-2 to VP-8 inclusive. On 17 September 1941 the serial was amended to the form SB-1 to SB-8, except VP-3, which had been destroyed earlier. Thus the confusing serial numbering was over, so far as captured bombers were concerned.

After the outbreak of the Continuation War sixteen SB bombers were bought from the German war booty depots. The aircraft were delivered in three lots, packed in crates. Six aircraft arrived on 5 November 1941 and they were given serials SB-9 to SB-14. The following five aircraft arrived on 11 April 1942 and received serials SB-15 to SB-19. The last batch came on 27 August 1942 (SB-20 to SB-24). A total of twenty-four SB aircraft were in the Finnish Air Force inventory.

Considering the circumstances in Finland a good number of SBs were purchased and the air force headquarters ordered on 7 September 1942 that SB-6 and SB-8 were to be modified as trainers. All armament was removed, the glass nose received a wooden cone, the aircraft was fitted with dual controls and a second cockpit was built in the observer's position. The dorsal gun position was covered with a sliding hatch. The modifications were carried out on SB-6 by 25 January 1943 and on SB-8 by 1 March 1943. In Soviet Union this modification was designated as USB.

Continuation War

The SB bombers were placed in *Lentolaivue* 6, which was attached to naval headquarters and was tasked with maritime reconnaissance, submarine search and attacks against Soviet naval detachments. At the beginning of the Continuation War on 25 June 1941 LLv 6 possessed three SB bombers in its 2nd Flight.

2/LLv 6 performed its first mission on 28 June, when one SB reconnoitred the route Paldiski-Tallinn-Loksha and observed twenty-three vessels.

Of the aircraft captured in the Winter War, the first Tupolev SB put into flying condition was VP-10, seen here at the depot in April 1940. Its precise type designation was SB with 2 M-103 engines. The aircraft was painted Light Grey overall. The wing insignia conforms with the 4/5th of the chord rule. (VL)

On 25 July *luutn.* Seppälä bombed with an SB aircraft a merchantman of about 4,000 tons near Pien-Tytärsaari. The vessel was sunk.

On 24 August 2/LLv 6 leader *kapt.* Ek's SB pair tried to bomb near Söderskär naval detachment. They were engaged in a fight with six Soviet Chaikas, but managed to escape.

During the autumn the flight flew many reconnaissance missions over the sea and Russian traffic from Hanko to the east was under special attention. On several bombing missions no serious damage was caused to the enemy shipping.

When 1942 began 2/LLv 6 possessed five airworthy SB bombers.

In March the flight reconnoitred and photographed Suursaari (Gogland) for the forthcoming invasion. On 27 March 1942 the battle started and *kapt.* Ek bombed installations on Suursaari, with four SBs hitting the targets. Four captured I-153 fighters of the squadron flew escort and then strafed the target area. The occupation was completed in the evening of the following day

After midnight on 28 May *luutn.* Virtanen made the first submarine observation from an SB on the east side of Suursaari. In the morning *luutn.* Palosuo dropped a depth charge from an SB on a submarine travelling in the same area at periscope depth.

After an explosion the submarine disappeared and lots of oil surfaced. Russian records confirm that submarine M-95 was destroyed at this time and place.

On 30 May the squadron commander gave an order for submarine search east of the Södeskär-Juminda line up to the meridian of Lavansaari.

Before midnight on 25 June *kapt.* Ek, near Pellinki, released a depth charge on a submarine travelling on the surface, but without a hit. Half an hour later Ek's pair returned to the same area and dropped one depth charge on a submarine still on the surface. The vessel disappeared due to the impact of the explosion and rose at a 45-degree angle. Then another charge was released and the vessel tossed about in the explosion and submerged stern first. Many large air bubbles and quantities of oil surfaced. The submarine was StS-406, which was damaged, but could continue its journey at the bottom of the Gulf of Finland, returning to Kronstadt on 6 August.

Before midnight on 26 June one SB dropped a depth charge on a submerging submarine west of Suursaari and another in its direction. Plenty of oil surfaced and the vessel was possibly damaged.

On 14 July in the afternoon luutn. Teräs dropped from an SB a depth charge outside Pellinki on a submarine travelling at periscope depth. A lot of oil surfaced. On the next mission three additional depth charges were dropped and mine ship Ruotsinsalmi was guided to the spot to release eleven more depth charges. Russian sources confirm that submarine StS-317 was destroyed.

VP-6 of 2/LLv 6 parked at Nummela, at the edge of the airfield. The aircraft joined its unit on 30 August 1941. Three days later the flight and squadron HQ moved to Helsinki Malmi. This plane came from later production batches, evidenced by the M-103Y engines with streamlined cooling intakes. (Finnish Air Force Museum)

On 18 August *kapt*. Ek's SB dropped two depth charges between Suursaari and Tyters on a semi-submerged submarine. Submarine StS-407 was damaged, but returned to its base on 28 September.

On 20 September *kapt*. Ek released from an SB a depth charge on a submarine travelling on the surface west of Suursaari. The vessel disappeared under the pillar of water created by the explosion and submerged. Plenty of oil surfaced and another depth charge more oil. Submarine S-12 was damaged.

On 22 September *kapt*. Ek dropped two depth charges on a submerging vessel outside Pellinki. On three separate missions another six depth charges were dropped and the patrol motorboats guided to the spot released a further six. Plenty of oil surfaced. The target was still S-12, but in spite of the damage it could continue its journey and returned to Kronstadt as late as 15 November.

On 30 September the 1st Flight received its first SB and in the next month another three. Its operational area consisted of the Aaland Sea and southern Bothnic Sea, starting missions a fortnight later, but with no submarines sighted.

2/LeLv 6 line-up at Malmi on 14 September 1942. From right are SB-1, 11, 8, 7, 10, 12 and 13. The flight was tasked with anti-submarine missions over the Gulf of Finland. The squadron abbreviation LeLv was introduced on 3 May 1942.

On 14 October *luutn.* Palosuo of 2/LeLv 6 in an SB in the western Gulf of Finland saw a semi-submerged vessel, which submerged in the attack. After the first depth charge, large air bubbles surfaced and after the second one oil bubbled to the surface along with more air bubbles. Russian records confirmed the loss of submarine StS-302.

On 16 November LeLv 6 was attached to the newly established *Lentorykmentti* 5, which flew for the commander of the navy. The tasks remained as before.

At the beginning of 1943 LeLv had three serviceable SB bombers in the 1st Flight and six more on the 2nd Flight.

On 7 February came an order to cease submarine searches and cut down flying to a minimum.

On 13 February the regiment was attached to the air force commander and LeLv 6 transferred the 2nd Flight on 19 February to Immola, to prepare for harassment bombardments of air bases located north of Leningrad.

Before midnight on 18 March one SB bombed Kasimovo and another Levashovo bases. Hits by the 500 kg bomb load were recorded on the fields.

SB-14 bomber of 2/LeLv 6 in winter camouflage at Immola in March 1943. The flight performed from here nocturnal harassment bombardments of Soviet airfields north of Leningrad. This plane had DN-väri undersides painted at the factory on 8 August 1942 with the Warpaint. (Paavo Saari)

SB-10 of 2/LeLv 6 at Utti on 17 September 1943, when kers. Erkki Vuorio flew it on a bombing mission to Lavansaari. The Warpaint was applied at the factory on 1 August 1942, using the splinter pattern specified for captured aircraft. (Aulis Bremer)

2/LeLv 6 leader kapt. Birger Ek takes off on 21 October 1943 from Malmi for the 1000th mission of his flight, in SB-10. Ek had earlier received the Mannerheim Cross for very successful anti-submarine warfare missions. (SA-kuva)

Before midnight on 21 March *kapt.* Ritjärvi bombed, with four aircraft, Levashovo, Kasimovo, Shuvalovo and Kapitolov bases. Hits were observed on the field and blast pens. Twenty-four hours later *luutn.* Haapanen with four SBs bombed Levashovo, Gorskaya and Uglovo bases, hitting the target areas. After midnight on 25 March one SB bombed Uglovo and another Levashovo base.

On 30 March the SBs returned to Malmi and the attachments were reverted.

On 14 April the regiment gave an order for submarine searches in the Gulf of Finland between Bogskär and Gogland. The Russian submarine movements were small, because the double anti-submarine net placed between Porkkala and Naissaari effectively prevented access of the vessels west of this line.

During the summer the 1st Flight flew only a few search missions and the 2nd Flight an average of two sorties per week, observing only streams of oil. Some depth charges were dropped, but no submarines were met or damaged.

On 13 September the squadron was tasked to participate in the aerial attack on Lavansaari air base, forming a group headed by *kapt.* Härmälä.

In the evening of 17 September five SBs of *kapt.* Härmälä took off for Lavansaari. Only three aircraft found the target, in poor weather, and dropped their bombs in the island. All aircraft returned to base.

By the end of the year the 1st Flight flew only two search sorties and the 2nd Flight carried out one sortie weekly, if the weather permitted. No submarine observations were recorded.

1944 began quietly with 13 serviceable SB bombers. On 14 February the squadron name was changed to *Pommituslentolaivue* 6 (PLeLv 6).

During the spring a number of uneventful search mission were flown, in addition to ice reconnaissance, anti-aircraft target and searchlight practise flights.

During the open water season the 1st Flight flew a search sortie every second or third day and the 2nd Flight one at dawn and another at dusk. The missions of the 1st Flight ceased on 6 June.

On 8 August an SB of the 2nd Flight flew the squadron's last mission in the Continuation War over the Gulf of Finland.

SB-6 of T-LeLv 17 at Luonetjärvi in March 1943. The modification to a trainer included the removal of all armament and adding a second cockpit in the navigator's position. The dorsal gun position had a sliding hatch instead of a turret. The other SB modified to a trainer was SB-8. (Klaus Niska coll.)

SB-6 of T-LeLv 17 returns from a training mission to Luonetjärvi on 31 March 1944. The Warpaint of Olive Green and Black with DN-väri undersides is shown clearly. (SA-kuva)

SB-6 of T-LeLv 17 is pushed back to the hangar at Luonetjärvi on 31 March 1944, showing clearly the contemporary standard paintwork. (SA-kuva)

On 4 September 1944 the cease-fire ended all hostilities between Finland and the Soviet Union.

The squadron had operated through the Continuation War with SB bombers in one to three flights. No SBs were lost in action; seven aircraft were destroyed in accidents or technical failures. One pilot and two observers were killed. The SBs had sunk two submarines (M-95, StS-302) and participated in the sinking on one more (StS-317). Additionally a large merchant ship and four smaller vessels were sunk.

Lapland War

According to the truce with the Soviet Union the Germans were to retreat from Finnish territory by 15 September 1944. Since the Germans did not withdraw their troops by the deadline, military actions were taken against them.

The task of *Pommituslentolaivue* 6, subordinated to *Lentorykmentti* 4, was specified as search for German submarines in the Aaland Sea, Bothnic Sea and western Gulf of Finland.

On 28 October one SB, searching for submarines in the Aaland Sea, flew the first mission in the Lapland War. Search sorties were flown twice or three times a day if the weather permitted.

SB-7 of 2/PLeLv 6 in flight on 3 June 1944, piloted by ylik. Aarne Korhonen on this occasion. Both the take-off and landing took place at Nummela. The Warpaint was factory applied on 16 March 1943. (SA-kuva)

SB bombers of 2/PLeLv 6 preparing for a submarine search mission at Nummela during the first week of June 1944. Above is SB-7 and below SB-23, both in same colour camouflage, but with different patterns. (SA-kuva)

SB-13 of 2/PLeLv 6 tried to take off from Nummela on 25 July 1944 with a locked rudder. The pilot shut the throttle and the plane went over the runway sideways onto its belly. (Finnish National Archives)

On 4 December the air force was demobilized and PLeLv 6 was disbanded. The 2nd Flight was transferred to PLeLv 45, forming its 2nd Flight. The tasks remained the same.

On 22 March 1945 the last mission by SBs was flown, when one aircraft searched for submarines on route Turku-Hanko-Utö-Bentskär-Turku, with no sightings.

In the Lapland War the SBs flew 84 submarine search sorties without any results. No aircraft were lost.

In February some of the aircraft were put into storage at the air depot and the remaining ones were flown there on 4 April 1945. The aircraft were removed from the air force records on 2 January 1950.

SB-7 of 2/PLeLv 6 searching for submarines over the Gulf of Finland on 3 June 1944, piloted by ylik. Aarne Korhonen. No sightings were made this season, as the double anti-submarine net between Porkkala and Tallinn did not permit the passage to west. (SA-kuva)

S/n	Delivered	Struck off charge	Remarks	Flying Hours
VP-10, VP-1, SB-1	11 Mar 1940	2 Jan 1950	Last flight 16 Feb 1945	397.15
VP-2, SB-2	15 Feb 1941	23 Jul 1942	W/o Malmi 6 Apr 1942	142.50
VP-3	3 Jul 1941	30 Aug 1941	W/o Nummela 2 Aug 1941	9.10
VP-4, SB-4	19 Mar 1941	19 Sep 1942	W/o Malmi 4 Aug 1942	202.40
SB-5	11 Mar 1942	2 Jan 1950	Last flight 16 Feb 1945	214.35
VP-6, SB-6	17 Aug 1941	2 Jan 1950	Last flight 23 Feb 1945	268.40
VP-7, SB-7	8 Aug 1941	2 Jan 1950	Last flight 6 Feb 1945	237.45
VP-8, SB-8	7 Apr 1941	9 Feb 1945	W/o Luonetjärvi 25 Oct 1944	289.40
SB-9	5 Nov 1941	2 Jan 1950	Last flight 20 Feb 1945	172.50
SB-10	5 Nov 1941	2 Jan 1950	Last flight 1 Feb 1945	356.30
SB-11	5 Nov 1941	13 Nov 1942	W/o Malmi 24 Sep 1942	72
SB-12	5 Nov 1941	2 Jan 1950	Last flight 13 Mar 1945	337.35
SB-13	5 Nov 1941	9 Oct 1944	W/o Nummela 25 Jul 1944	338.40
SB-14	5 Nov 1941	2 Jan 1950	Last flight 23 Feb 1945	313.05
SB-15	11 Apr 1942	15 Dec 1942	W/o Pori 14 Oct 1942	5.25
SB-16	11 Apr 1942	2 Jan 1950	Last flight 15 Feb 1945	173.25
SB-15	11 Apr 1942	2 Jan 1950	Last flight 4 Apr 1945	195.05
SB-18	11 Apr 1942	2 Jan 1950	Last flight 4 Apr 1945	144.40
SB-19	11 Apr 1942	2 Jan 1950	Last flight 16 Feb 1945	218
SB-20	27 Aug 1942	2 Jan 1950	Last flight 4 Apr 1945	104.35
SB-21	27 Aug 1942	2 Jan 1950	Last flight 24 Feb 1945	126.15
SB-22	27 Aug 1942	16 Sep 1943	W/o Malmi 6 Jul 1943	37.50
SB-23	27 Aug 1942	2 Jan 1950	Last flight 9 Feb 1945	83.25
SB-24	27 Aug 1942	2 Jan 1950	W/o Tampere 23 Feb 1945	20.50

SB pair of PLeLv 6 on its way on 21 October 1944 from Nummela to Pori, from where submarine searches were flown against the Germans. The closer plane is SB-20. Yellow eastern front markings were painted over a month earlier. (Finnish Air Force).

Tupolev SB
Camouflage and markings

The first of the eight captured Tupolev SB bombers, serialled VP-10, received an overall Light Grey paint at the factory.

Warpaint was introduced on 30 September 1940 and it consisted of Olive Green and Black upper surfaces with aluminium lacquer undersides for metal covered aircraft. The other seven SBs under repair at the factory were painted in this scheme, beginning with VP-2 on 5 February 1941.

The sixteen SBs (SB-9–24) bought from German war booty depots all received Warpaint, SB-9 being the first on 10 July 1942. The pattern was the regular wavy one for SB-9, 10 and 11, but from SB-12 onwards the splinter pattern for captured aircraft was used. Also, all these aircraft received the *DN-väri* undersides, which was introduced on 7 May 1942.

The sinking markings and missions flown by 2/Lentolaivue 6 were marked on the tail of Tupolev SB serialled VP-3, starting from 15 July 1941. This aircraft stalled at take off from Nummela on 2 August 1941 and crashed in the forrest. (Kari Stenman coll.)

Eight Tupolev SBs, which were captured in the Winter War, were put into service with the Finnish Air Force. The first one was VP-10 seen here at the air depot in April 1940, wearing an overall Light Grey colour. (VL)

The SB was the only other bomber type in addition to the Dornier Do 17 Z, which received white winter camouflage. This was applied in February 1943 to the four aircraft (SB-9, 12, 13 and 14), which were assigned to the attacks against Leningrad area airfields.

Of the older aircraft, SB-8 was the first to get the splinter type Warpaint with *DN-väri* undersides on 22 August 1942, followed later in the year by SB-5, 6, 1 and 9 in chronological order. These colour were worn on the SBs until the end of their flying career in April 1945.

SB-9 of 2/LeLv 6 at Helsinki Malmi in April 1943. The white winter was was applied to half a dozen SBs of the flight, which was tasked with harassment bombing of Leningrad area airfields during the second half of March 1943. (Kari Stenman coll.)

Tupolev SB, VP-8, luutn. Unto Seppälä, 2/Lentolaivue 6, Nummela airfield, July 1941. Camouflage colours: upper surfaces Olive Green and Black, under surfaces aluminium dope. Standard Eastern Front markings Yellow, serial Black, Sinking markings White.

VP-8 of 2/LLv 6 at Nummela in July 1941. The designation of the bomber is SB with 2 M-100 engines. Right photo shows the sinking marks of luutn. Unto Seppälä's VP-8 in 1941. The dates are the 22.7 (2,000 tons), 24.7 (4,000 tons) and 25.7 (4,000 tons). (Kari Stenman coll.)

136

Tupolev SB, SB-1, luutn. Erkki Palosuo, 2/Lentolaivue 6, Malmi airfield, September 1942. Camouflage colours: upper surfaces Olive Green and Black, under surfaces aluminium dope. Standard Eastern Front markings Yellow, serial Black and Olive Green, Sinking markings Yellow.

SB-1 of 2/LeLv 6 at the head of a line-up at Malmi on 14 September 1942. The regular pilot was luutn. Erkki Palosuo. At right is the tail of SB-1, wearing a wreath around the flight badge at Malmi on 21 October 1943. The submarine sinking dates were 28.5.42, 16.6.42, 25.6.42 and 14.10.42. This plane received splinter pattern Warpaint on 8 May 1943. (Finnish Air Force)

137

Tupolev SB, SB-9, kapt. Birger Ek, flight leader of 2/Lentolaivue 6, Malmi airfield, October 1942. Camouflage colours: upper surfaces Olive Green and Black, under surfaces DN-väri. Standard Eastern Front markings Yellow, serial Black and Olive Green. Sinking markings Yellow.

SB-9 of 2/LeLv 6 leader kapt. Ek parked at Helsinki Malmi in spring 1943, surrounded by the flight personnel. To the right is the crew, from the left gunner vääp. Toivo Peltonen, pilot kapt. Birger Ek and observer luutn. Niilo Halla. (SA-kuva)

Tupolev SB, SB-9, kapt. Birger Ek, flight leader of 2/Lentolaivue 6, Malmi airfield, October 1942.

Tupolev SB, SB-5, Täydennyslentolaivue 17, Luonetjärvi airfield, March 1943. Camouflage colours: upper surfaces Olive Green and Black, under surfaces DN-väri. Standard Eastern Front markings Yellow, serial Black and Olive Green.

SB-5 of T-LeLv 17 at Luonetjärvi in March 1943. The second and now splinter type of regulation Warpaint with DN-väri undersides was applied on 28 November 1942 during an accident repair at the factory. (Kari Stenman coll.)

Tupolev SB, SB-5, Täydennyslentolaivue 17, Luonetjärvi airfield, March 1943.

141

Tupolev SB, SB-5, Täydennyslentolaivue 17, Luonetjärvi airfield, March 1943. Camouflage colours: upper surfaces Olive Green and Black, under surfaces DN-väri. Standard Eastern Front markings Yellow, serial Black and Olive Green.

SB-5 after repair at the factory at Tampere in January 1943. The cause of the damage was a stall landing, and the time spent at the factory was seven months. The aircraft was fitted with an MV-2 ventral turret under fuselage. It was one of four so equipped, the others being SB-2, 11 and 19. (Aaretti Nieminen)

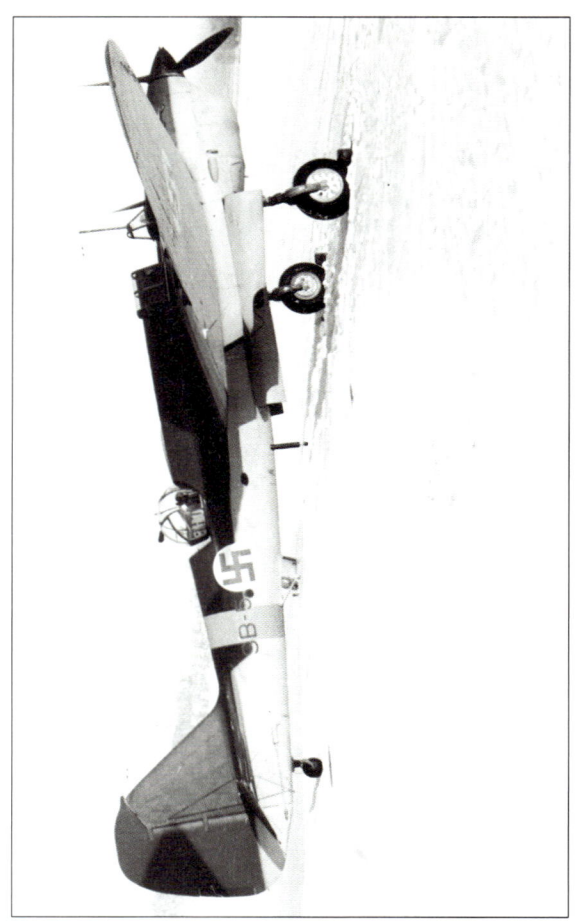

Tupolev SB, SB-14, ylikers. Aarne Korhonen, 2/Lentolaivue 6, Malmi airfield, May 1944. Camouflage colours: upper surfaces Olive Green and Black, under surfaces DN-väri. Standard Eastern Front markings Yellow, serial Olive Green and Black.

SB-14 of 2/LeLv 6 at Malmi on 20 May 1943. It was usually flown by ylikers. Aarne Korhonen. The aircraft carries the splinter type Warpaint with DN-väri underside, painted at the factory on 8 August 1942. (Finnish Air Force).

Tupolev SB, SB-13, kers. Erkki Vuorio, 2/Lentolaivue 6, Immola airfield, March 1943. Camouflage colours: upper surfaces White winter wash, under surfaces DN-väri. Standard Eastern Front markings Yellow, serial Black and Ollive Green.

SB-13 bomber of 2/LeLv 6 in winter camouflage at Immola in March 1943. The regular pilot was kers. Erkki Vuorio. The flight carried out nocturnal harassment bombardments of airfields north of Leningrad. (Paavo Saari)

144

Tupolev SB, SB-13, kers. Erkki Vuorio, 2/Lentolaivue 6, Immola airfield, March 1943.

Dornier Do 17 Z

The Finnish bomber force suffered heavy losses during the Finnish advance in the summer and autumn of 1941. A welcome reinforcement was received from Germany, when the German *Reichsmarschall* Hermann Göring donated, on 11 November 1941, fifteen Dornier Do 17 Z bombers and 300,000 kg bombs to Finland. Not a great sacrifice, as the type was being phased out from operational serviced in the *Luftwaffe*.

Finnish aircrews picked up the bombers in several lots and the first arrived in Finland on 5 January and the last on 11 February 1942. Finnish serials DN-51 to DN-65 inclusive and national insignia were painted on in Finland.

Dornier Do 17 Z-3, serial DN-54, of 3/LLv 46 at Linnunniemi near Joensuu in February 1942. The squadron badge depicted a European bison in a shield and was said to represent the squadron CO maj. Reino Artola. (Finnish Air Force Museum)

3/LLv 46 leader kapt. Tauno Meller paid a visit to Luonetjärvi with DN-54 on 6 April 1942. The original German upper surface RLM greens 70 and 71 received a white winter wash on 11 February 1942. The lower surfaces remained in RLM 65. (Otto Rautanen)

Continuation War

On 2 April 1942 *ev.luutn.* Olavi Sarko was appointed as the new commander of *Lentorykmentti* 4. LLv 46 had completed training with the Dorniers and the squadron was declared operational. Due to the strong Russian flak and fighter threat it was decided to fly missions under the cover of darkness: take-off at night, bombing at dawn and return in daylight. Also the full power of the whole regiment was exploited in concentrated strikes.

On 5 April LeR 4 carried out the first joint operation by all three squadrons. The target was the most important Soviet air base in Karelia, Segesha, which was extended in winter to the nearby Lake Akanjärvi's ice. Twenty-one aircraft took off for the mission and just before 5am *maj.* Artola's eight Dorniers of LLv 46 bombed (160x50 kg) from 1,200–1,300 m. Part of the bomb salvo hit the blast pen row, part 50–100 m east of it on the ice and on the shore.

On 13 April LLv 46 bombed at the dawn the headquarters of a Russian division in the village of Vonozero, south of Podporoze. with nine Dorniers of *kapt.* Jussi Räty The bombs exploded in the target area, direct hits were scored on several buildings, a few fires were lit and several black columns of black smoke rose after the attack.

147

Do 17 Z-3 DN-53 of 3/LeLv 46 paid a visit to Utti on 4 September 1942. The Warpaint was unit applied on 6 May 1942, retaining its RLM 65 undersides. This plane is one of two which had the serial painted in black, the other being DN-51. (Olli Riekki)

Two days later LeR 4 participated in repelling a Soviet infantry offensive at the central River Svir by bombing warehouse and camp areas. The whole regiment made a nocturnal attack against the Varbinitsy supply center with 19 bombers. At 5am *kapt.* Meller's nine Dorniers of LLv 46 bombed from 1,300 m, dropping 180x50 kg bombs. All but eight bombs hit the target area. After the bombardment fires were seen in the middle of the target, visible as far away as the River Svir.

When aerial reconnaissance discovered that several barges had passes the winter at the mouths of the rivers Vodla and Andoma running into Lake Onega, the task to destroy these was given to LeR 4 and LeR 2, in addition to the saw mill at the river Vodla.

LeR 4 was ordered to attack on 9 May with all forces simultaneously both targets and repeat the attack as quickly as possible. The first bombardment would be made without fighter escort and on the second mission the fighters of LeR 2 would fly as escort. LeLv 46 would attack both times from Joensuu to the mouth of the river Andoma located 50 km to the south.

LeLv 46 bombed the mouth of the river Andoma just before seven in the morning with ten Dorniers, and repeated the attack at three in the afternoon with 11 Dorniers with an escort of six Brewsters from Nurmoila. As a whole the results were modest.

DN-56 of 3/LeLv 46 photographed at Petrozavodsk airfield Solomanni on 8 June 1942. Solitary planes flew guerilla drop missions behind Lake Onega. On this occasion the pilot was ylik. Eino Holmgren. The Warpaint was applied on 28 April 1942. (Esko Rinne)

In the town of Segesha, located on the west bank of Lake Uikujärvi, was a gun factory, sulphuric acid factory and cellulose mill plus a power plant. These in addition to a noteworthy air base were often the targets of LeR 4. The next blow by the whole regiment was carried out on 31 August, this time on the air base. In all 22 bombers took off headed for the target.

LeLv 46 flew with *kapt.* Erkki Uotinen's eight Dorniers, bombing at 4am from 1,400 m. Bombs (160x50 kg) hit the west edge of the airfield, partly in the aircraft shelters and through the warehouse area. A larger fire in the centre of the edge of the airfield was observed.

On 23 November 1942 LeLv 46 attacked in the evening the air base at Segesha with three Dornier pairs. The target was the runway, aircraft and a building south-west of it. The bombing took place in the evening and most of the bombs were seen to hit the target, but darkness prevented accurate observations.

The bombardment of Segesha armament factories had been postponed several times, but it began to emerge that an attack by the whole regiment could be made on 19 February 1943. It was decided to carry this out at 17.00 by 18 aircraft of four squadrons.

*Do 17 Z-3 DN-58 of
2/LeLv 46 on a visit to
Nurmoila on 8 May 1942,
piloted by the squadron
CO, maj. Reino Artola.
The plane wears very neat
Warpaint applied only two
days earlier. Otherwise
it carries quite standard
markings. (Finnish Air
Force)*

Of *kapt*. Otto Rautanen's LeLv 46 five Dornier detachment, three planes were separated after take-off from the group and they found the target. At 22.20–22.40 they bombed Segesha supply and storage centre from 100–800 m altitude, with 5x250 kg and 50x50 kg bombs, which caused a large fire. On the return they faced a snow storm over the border. Only the lead aircraft landed at Joensuu. DN-53 crashed at Eno and DN-65 on the ice of Lake Kaltimojärvi. DN-56 was damaged in a forced landing at Lentiera and DN-59 crashed at Kuutamolahti. Five crew members were killed.

During the spring and summer the crippled LeLv 46 flew a few bombing missions with small forces of three or four Dorniers against targets south of the River Svir.

On 20 August LeR 4 flew a joint bombing mission targeting the Eastern Karelian village of Lehto, where a large partisan supply and raining base was located. Thirty-one bombers went to the target escorted by twelve Moranes.

Do 17 Z-1 coded DN-59 of 3/LeLv 46 on a visit to Luonetjärvi on 5 August 1942. The pilot on this occasion was kapt. *Tauno Meller, who then took a post at LeR 4 headquarters. The Warpaint was unit applied exactly three months earlier. (Finnish Aviation Museum)*

Six Dorniers led by *kapt.* Rautanen bombed from 600 m, with 90x50 kg bombs. Hits were observed on houses on both sides of the road, with at least nine destroyed. Several fires were lit.

The evening of September 17 seemed like a good moment for LeR 4 to attack. Lavansaari was to be bombed with 30 planes between 20.15–21.55 and again between 03.00–04.00. Order of attack was LeLv 6, 48, 42, 46 and 44, all from different directions and altitudes. Haze appeared over the Gulf of Finland, causing a one hour delay and expectations of a recall, which did not happen.

Now it was LeLv 46 led by *maj.* Reino Artola with six Dorniers. Three planes were separated from the rest in the haze, dropped their bombs into Lake Ladoga, and returned to Mensuvaara. One plane missed Lavansaari and dropped its bombs into a lake. Two planes located Lavansaari and bombed it at 22.00, but did not see any results due to haze and flak. All planes returned safely to Mensuvaara. The second strike was called off.

In February 1944 the ADD, long distance bombing unit of the Russians, bombed Helsinki with strong forces on three nights, 6/7., 16/17. and 26/27 of February. The planes flew from fields around Leningrad, where the Finnish reconnaissance missions had noted dozens of planes on each site. The fields were fully lit at take-off and landing times, and thus were good targets for bombing. So *Lentorykmentti* 4 ordered PLeLv 46 to attack these sites with full squadron strength.

On 29 February PLeLv 46 tried a new tactical trick. In the evening, *luutn.* Erkki Jaakkola took off with his four Dorniers, staggered in altitude. Over the Gulf of Finland, the Dorniers infiltrated the returning Soviet formations and flew with them to Levashovo. At 22.25–23.10 they bombed the fully lit field, where many planes were landing. The bombs hit the rows of planes and hangars, and the landing planes. Many fires were lit and a very powerful explosion shook the field. AA opened up only as the planes left.

On 2 March LeR 4 was ordered to bomb Russian airfields on the Karelian Isthmus with all squadrons. Finnish bombers were to join the returning Russian bomber fleets and bomb the fields, usually well lit, at landing time. Results proved rather good.

On 9 March LeR 4 was given a new chance to infiltrate an ADD bombing mission returning from Tallinn. Over the Gulf of Finland, the Finns joined the formations and flew to their bases. PLeLv 46 blended in with the Russians west of Kronstadt, with *kapt.* Onni Pesola's five Dorniers bound for Levashovo, bombing at 21.34 from 1,400 m. Hits were scored on the runway and in the immediate vicinity of the rows of planes.

Do 17 Z-3 DN-60 of 1/LeLv 46 at Noljakka in June 1942. The occasion was the taking of recognition pictures for the manuals. The supports served to imitate in flight views. The Warpaint was applied on 6 May 1942 in a very standard manner. The aircraft bellied on 25 August 1942, was sent to Germany for repairs, but never came back. (Finnish Air Force)

Both photos: Do 17 Z-3 DN-64 of LeLv 46 at Tiiksjärvi. From there it flew a photographic mission on 13 January 1943. The aircraft had retained its cartography cameras from the previous summer season. It can also be identified by the playing card emblem on the nose. The assigned pilot at this point was vääp. *Oiva Eerola. DN-64 was the only one of its type to receive a white wash in this winter, applied on 10 December 1942. (SA-kuva)*

On 3 April LeR 4 concentrated 34 planes for an attack on the airfield at Kähy, northeast of Leningrad. Aerial reconnaissance had found 57 planes there the day before. PLeLv 46 came in last with six planes, including four Dorniers led by *luutn.* Jaakkola, bombing the target from 3,300 m. Hits were recorded next to the revetments east and north-east of the field. Six fires were lit. On leaving the area, 23 fires were counted, with three major ones. One large explosion occurred, starting a fire.

After the ground thaw was over, the airfield of Mergino at the mouth of the River Svir became a target once more. On 19 May LeR 4 took off with 42 planes, 41 of which bombed the base right after midnight. This was the biggest number of planes the regiment ever managed to get to the target.

Luutn. Jaakkola and his six PLeLv 46 Dorniers bombed the target from 1,500 m just after midnight. Hits were observed in target area and at least three fires lit. Many incendiary fires were also seen.

After the success achieved against Germany in the spring of 1944, the Soviet Union began in the Karelian Isthmus the fourth of ten strategic efforts. This was to be the only one which did not reach its goals. The offensive started on the 9 June 1944, and on the next day the first Finnish line of defence was breached, forcing the Finns to retreat. LeR 4 was given an order to prepare for an all-out attack in the Karelian Isthmus. To avoid losses and spare the sparse resources, the regiment ordered attacks to take place primarily at night. Russian breakthroughs forced the air forces to act without regard to losses.

Rainy weather had prevented bombing operations, but on 11 June PLeLv 46 faced dismal weather and attacked the forces advancing from Mainila with six Dorniers, led by *kapt.* Ilpo Tuominen. Russian flak shot down half of the planes, four crew members were killed, four went missing, and three were wounded.

During the hectic battles of summer 1944 PLeLv 46 participated in all but one of the 25 full regiment bombing attacks on the Karelian Isthmus and north of Lake Ladoga. The strength was an average of three Dorniers on each mission.

On 9 August PLeLv 46 had its final war mission when the last regimental bombing effort was sent to attack the Suojärvi station with 30 planes. The goal was to disrupt the retreat. The planes went in two waves, escorted by six Messerschmitts. In the second wave was PLeLv 46 with five aircraft, including one Dornier.

PLeLv 46 had flown 415 sorties with the Dorniers, six aircraft were lost in action and another four in flying accidents. Twenty airmen were killed or captured.

On 4 September 1944 the commander of the Air Force ordered the air regiments to tell squadrons to cease fighting at 7.00. A ceasefire commenced and two weeks later it was confirmed by the Moscow Armistice.

Lapland War

On 4 September the Air Force set up the Special Staff Sarko, with *ev.* Olavi Sarko commanding, to run the air war in Lapland. *Lentorykmentti* 2 and LeR 4 were ordered to prepare to participate.

PLeLv 46 had only three Dorniers remaining and one or two of these flew on most LeR 4 missions against the retreating German troops.

On 4 April 1945 DN-55 took off on a photo mission to Kilpisjärvi. The plane returned to Kemi at 16.00. This was the last war mission of the Finnish Air Force.

Do 17 Z-3 DN-55 of 1/LeLv 46 at Immola in May 1943, frequently piloted by luutn. Reino Lampelto. The markings are exactly as specified for the type, the Warpaint being applied on 6 May 1942. This machine has ejector type exhausts. (Reino Lampelto)

S/n	Werke Nummer	Delivered	Struck off charge	Remarks	Flying Hours
DN-51	3323	5 Jan 1942	9 Oct 1944	W/o Loimola 1 Aug 1944	342.30
DN-52	2608	6 Jan 1942	1 Oct 1952	Into storage 15 Sep 1948	296.40
DN-53	4242	6 Jan 1942	8 Apr 1943	W/o Eno 19 Feb 1943	147.50
DN-54	2856	13 Jan 1942	9 Oct 1944	W/o Kivannapa 11 Jun 1944	288.25
DN-55	3498	13 Jan 1942	1 Oct 1952	W/o Luonetjärvi 22 May 1947	418
DN-56	3425	29 Jan 1942	9 Oct 1944	W/o Kivennapa 11 Jun 1944	360.15
DN-57	1155	29 Jan 1942	11 Dec 1952	Into storage 24 Jul 1946	353.50
DN-58	2905	13 Jan 1942	1 Oct 1952	Last flight 13 Sep 1948	270.40
DN-59	3228	5 Jan 1942	9 Sep 1944	W/o Vegarusjärvi 26 Jul 1944	228.35
DN-60	2818	29 Jan 1942	11 Jan 1945	W/o Hirvas 25 Aug 1942	46.55
DN-61	4187	29 Jan 1942	9 Oct 1944	W/o Kivennapa 11 Jun 1944	291.15
DN-62	1218	11 Feb 1942	9 Jan 1943	W/o Liperi 23 May 1942	47.25
DN-63	2873	13 Jan 1942	9 Sep 1944	W/o Tali 30 Jun 1944	300.40
DN-64	2622	6 Jan 1942	1 Oct 1952	Into storage 15 Sep 1948	486,50
DN-65	1175	5 Jan 1942	16 Jul 1943	W/o Kaltimojärvi 19 Feb 1943	95.30

DN-57 of 1/PLeLv 46 parked at Kemi in late October 1944. It was regularly flown by the squadron CO, kapt. Olavi Pesola. The cylinders under the engines are heaters working with blow torches. The yellow eastern front markings were painted out by mid-September 1944 according to the cease-fire terms. (Reino Lampelto)

DN-55 of PLeLv 43 became low on fuel and landed at Kiiruna, Sweden on 7 March 1945. After filling the tanks kapt. *Jorma Turpeinen took off and flew back to Kemi. The Warpaint and subdued insignia were factory painted on 27 September 1944. At this point the yellow markings had been removed. (Mikael Forslund coll.)*

Dornier Do 17 Z
Camouflage and markings

On arrival in early 1942 most of the fifteen Dorniers were in original RLM camouflage of *Schwartzgrün* RLM 70 and *Dunkelgrün* RLM 71 with *Hellblau* RLM 65 undersides. These planes received at the air depot a winter camouflage, where usually the darker green (70) area was covered with white.

With other aircraft coming in German winter camouflage, only two aircraft, DN-51 and DN-53, were repainted into Warpaint at the air depot. The former also received aluminium dope undersides, which was according to contemporary regulations. Over the Warpaint was applied a white wash, either covering the black or random areas.

By 6 May 1942 the white was removed from the Dorniers and those still in German colours received new Warpaint, with *DN-väri* undersides.

Later, due to flying accidents, five Dorniers were repaired at the factory, which applied the second Warpaint, starting with DN-59 on 20 August 1943. The rest were repainted next year, chronologically DN-56, 64, 51 and 55. These colours remained on the aircraft until September 1948, when all bombers were put into storage and later scrapped.

DN-58 of 2/LeLv 46 on a visit to Nurmoila on 8 May 1942. The standard Warpaint pattern can be seen to some extent. The colours are Black and Olive Green upper surfaces and RLM 65 lower surfaces with yellow eastern front markings. (Finnish Air Force)

Six Dorniers of LeLv 46 in a line-up at Luonetjärvi in early May 1942. From the camera are DN-63, 65, 55 and 51. By 6 May 1942 all Dorniers had been painted into the Warpaint of Olive Green and Black with RLM 65 remaining underneath. (Kari Stenman coll.)

DN-64 of LeLv 46 during a photographic mission at Tiiksjärvi on 13 January 1943. The playing card emblem dates back to the previous summer, when each of the four planes of the Photoflight/LeLv 48 had an ace on the nose. (SA-Kuva)

DN-57 of 1/LeLv 46 at the dry beach at Noljakka in summer 1942. The paintwork complies fully with all regulations, the Warpaint being applied on 6 May 1942. (Finnish Air Force)

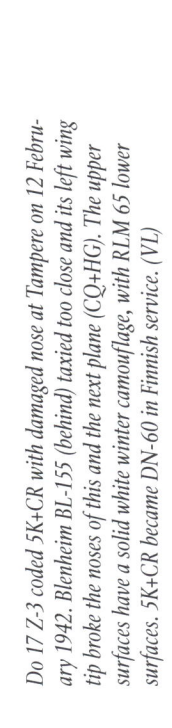

Dornier Do 17 Z-3, 5K+CR (DN-60) in ferry markings, Tampere airfield, February 1942. Camouflage colours: upper surfaces White, under surfaces Hellblau RLM 65. Standard Eastern Front markings Yellow.

W.Nr. 2818

Do 17 Z-3 coded 5K+CR with damaged nose at Tampere on 12 February 1942. Blenheim BL-155 (behind) taxied too close and its left wing tip broke the noses of this and the next plane (CQ+HG). The upper surfaces have a solid white winter camouflage, with RLM 65 lower surfaces. 5K+CR became DN-60 in Finnish service. (VL)

Dornier Do 17 Z-3, DN-60, kapt. Lassi Räty, leader of 1/Lentolaivue 46, Noljakka landing ground, June 1942. Camouflage colours: upper surfaces Olive Green and Black, under surfaces DN-väri. Standard Eastern Front markings Yellow, serial White.

DN-60 of 1/LeLv 46 at Noljakka in June 1942. The supports served to pose the aircraft as if in flight, for the photographer. The Warpaint was applied on 6 May 1942 in a standard manner. The plane's career in Finland ended on 25 August 1942 in a belly landing. The bomber was sent to Germany for repairs, but never came back. (Finnish Air Force)

Dornier Do 17 Z-3, DN-55, vänr. Olli Kepsu, 2/Lentolaivue 46, Linnunniemi landing ground, February 1942.
Camouflage colours: upper surfaces Schwartzgrün RLM 70 and Dunkelgrün RLM 71. Dark Green with White
covering most of 71 areas, under surfaces Hellblau RLM 65. Standard Eastern Front markings Yellow, serial White.

DN-55 of 2/LLv 46 on a short visit to Luonetjärvi on 27 February 1942. Luutn. Lassi Räty flew the plane back to Linnunniemi the same day. The white winter wash on this plane consisted mainly of the covering of the lighter RLM 71 areas. (Otto Rautanen)

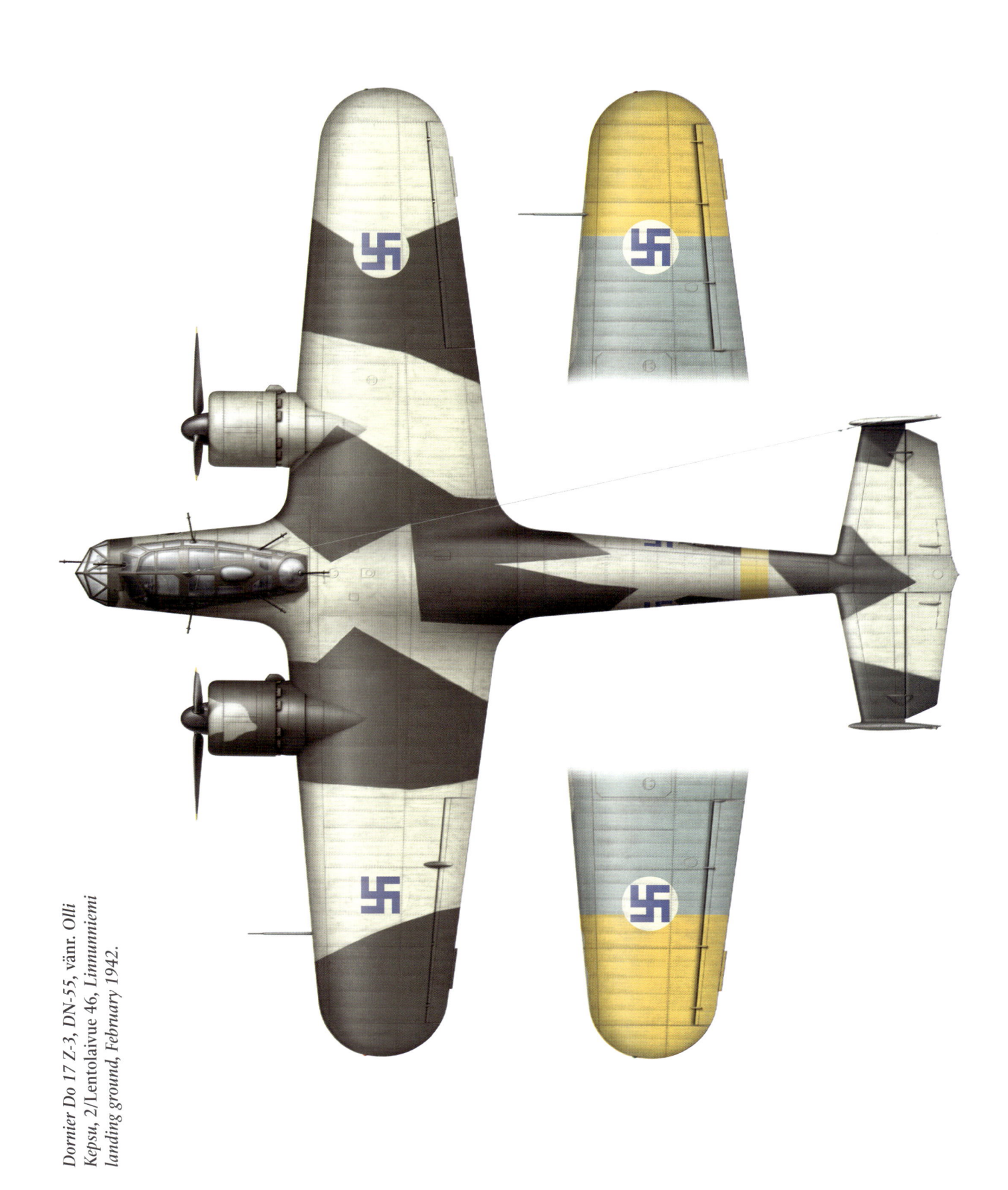

Dornier Do 17 Z-3, DN-55, vänr. Olli Kepsu, 2/Lentolaivue 46, Linnunniemi landing ground, February 1942.

Dornier Do 17 Z-3, DN-53, ltm. Toivo Parikka, 3/Lentolaivue 46, Linnunniemi landing ground, February 1942. Camouflage colours: upper surfaces Olive Green and Black with White covering most of black areas, under surfaces RLM 65. Standard Eastern Front markings Yellow, serial Black.

DN-53 was the first Dornier to arrive at Linnunniemi on 5 February 1942. It was posted to 3/LLv 46 and assigned to ltm Toivo Parikka. On arrival in Finland it wore German winter camouflage, which was covered with the Warpaint keeping the RLM 65 undersides, with some patchwork. The white winter wash was applied on this in irregular areas, all this during the course of January 1942. (Finnish Air Force Museum)

162

Dornier Do 17 Z-3, DN-53, ltm. Toivo Parikka, 3/Lentolaivue 46, Linnunniemi landing ground, February 1942.

Dornier Do 17 Z-3, DN-53, ltm. Toivo Parikka, 3/Lentolaivue 46, Linnunniemi landing ground, February 1942.

DN-53 of 3/LLv 46 from the other side. The white winter wash did not follow the colour divisions of the Warpaint. Other peculiarities with this plane were the white propeller spinners instead of the typical black. Also the serial was originally black, only on this machine and DN-51. (Otto Rautanen)

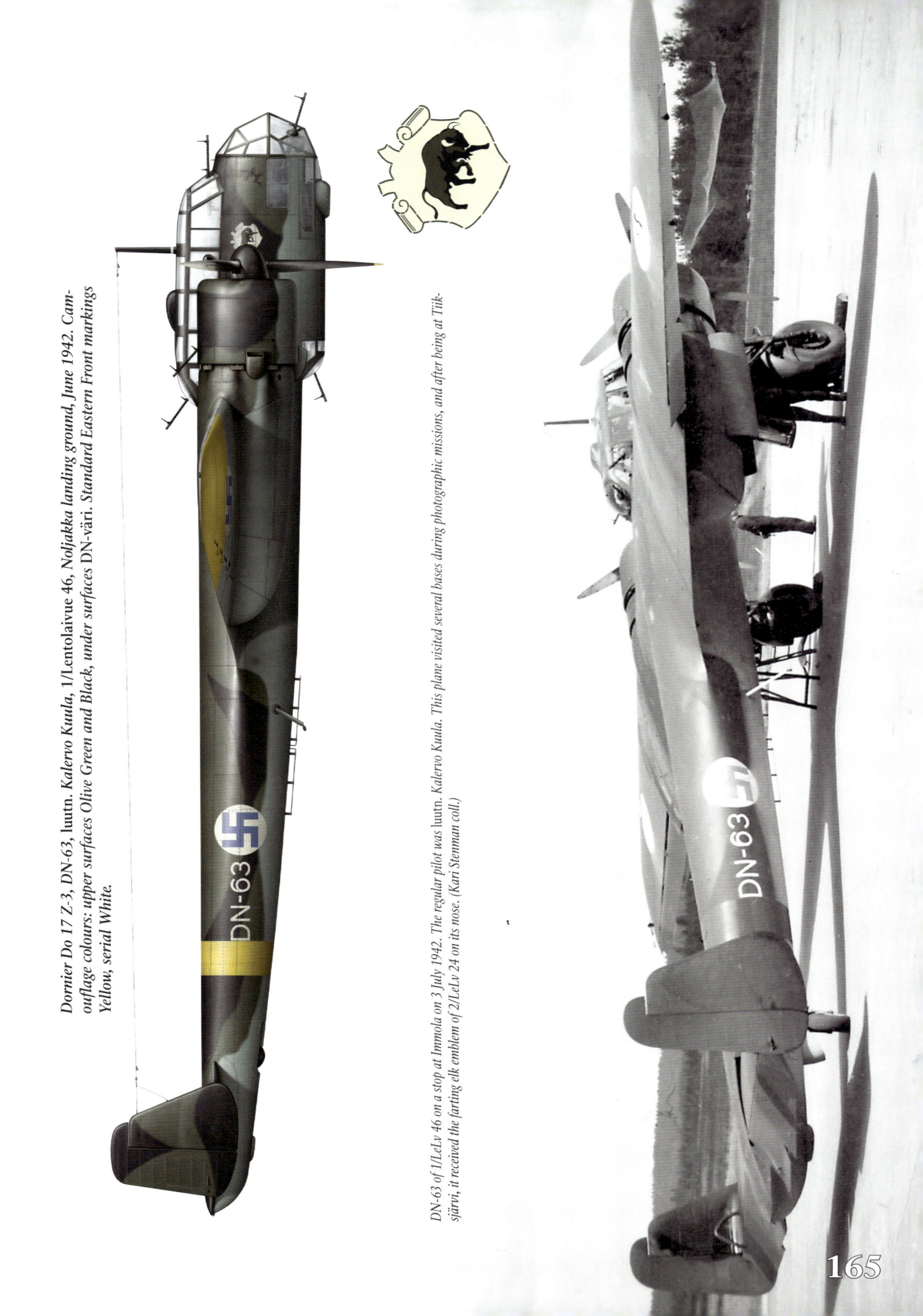

Dornier Do 17 Z-3, DN-63, luutn. Kalervo Kuula, 1/Lentolaivue 46, Noljakka landing ground, June 1942. Camouflage colours: upper surfaces Olive Green and Black, under surfaces DN-väri. Standard Eastern Front markings Yellow, serial White.

DN-63 of 1/LeLv 46 on a stop at Immola on 3 July 1942. The regular pilot was luutn. Kalervo Kuula. This plane visited several bases during photographic missions, and after being at Tiiksjärvi, it received the farting elk emblem of 2/LeLv 24 on its nose. (Kari Stenman coll.)

165

Dornier Do 17 Z-1, DN-51, kapt. Onni Pesola, leader of 2/Lentolaivue 46, Noljakka landing ground, October 1942. Camouflage colours: upper surfaces Olive Green and Black, under surfaces aluminium dope. Standard Eastern Front markings Yellow, serial Black.

Above: LeLv 46 airmen at Immola on 7 September 1943 in front of DN-51. From left luutn. Juhani Aitasalo, 2nd Flight leader kapt. Jussi Räty, squadron CO maj. Reino Artola and vänr. Erkki Puustinen. (Eino Ritaranta coll.)

Left: Dorniers of 2/LeLv 46 during formation flying over Joensuu on 22 November 1942. The closer DN-51 was the only one receiving the aluminium lacquer underside, appearing much darker that the RLM 65 under DN-55. (SA-kuva)

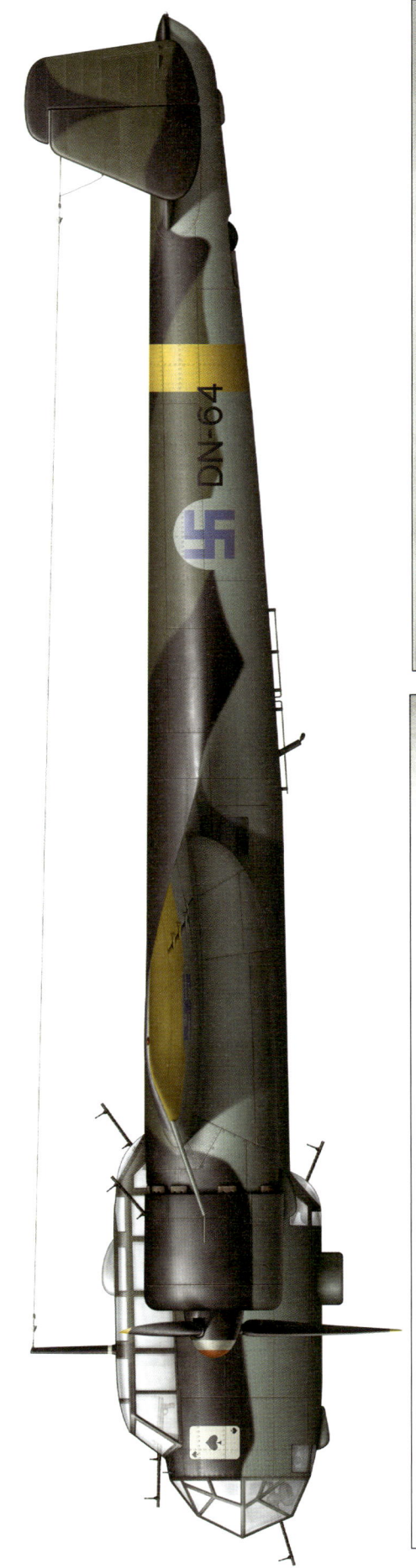

Dornier Do 17 Z-3, DN-64, ltm. Viljo Salminen, Pommituslentolaivue 48, Vaasa airfield, August 1944. Camouflage colours: upper surfaces Olive Green and Black, under surfaces DN-väri. Standard Eastern Front markings Yellow, serial Black.

DN-64 of the detached photo-flight of PLeLv 48 in summer 1944, left at Luonetjärvi and right at Vaasa. Also in this season the plane was assigned to ltm. Viljo Salminen. The flight identification was Red-White-Black spinners. The second Warpaint and subdued insignia were painted on 2 April 1944. (Lauri Bergman)

Dornier Do 17 Z-3, DN-64, ltm. Viljo Salminen, Pommituslentolaivue 48, Vaasa airfield, August 1944.

DN-64 parked next to Gauntlet GT-397 at Vaasa. Ltm. Salminen flew the plane there on 30 July and back to Onttola on 2 August 1944. The ace of spades playing card is now bigger that during the earlier photographic seasons. Also exceptional is the Black serial. (Lauri Bergman)

Dornier Do 17 Z-3, DN-64, ltm. Viljo Salminen, Pommituslentolaivue 48, Vaasa airfield, August 1944.

Petlyakov Pe-2 & Pe-3

After the outbreak of the Continuation War six Pe-2 aircraft were bought from the German war booty depots. The intention was to fly them to Finland from Pińsk, in eastern Poland, but the planes had received some combat damage and they were shipped on 19 December 1941.

The aircraft arrived at the aircraft factory on 10 January 1942, where they were refurbished and given serials PE-211 to PE-216.

The next aircraft was captured on 28 November 1942 and sent to the factory for repairs. This Pe-3 assault version was serialled PE-301. The last Pe-2 aircraft was bought from German was booty depots and delivered to the air force in Olomouc, Czechoslovakia, on 17 January 1944. It was flown to Finland, arriving on 29 January and later serialled PE-217. Thus the Finnish Air Force had a total of eight Pe-2s and Pe-3 aircraft in its inventory.

Pe-2 serial PE-212 of 1/LeLv 48 at Utti in August 1942. Training took place at Utti, until 4 September 1942, when the unit moved to Onttola. All Pe-2s received at the factory the splinter pattern Warpaint with DN-väri lower surfaces, as regulated on 7 May 1942. (Pauli Ervi)

Continuation War

Lentolaivue 48 was established at Luonetjärvi on 23 November 1941 under *Lentorykmentti* 4. *Maj.* J. Harju-Jeanty was appointed in command of the squadron. The task of LLv 48 was the advanced training of personnel for the regiment's needs.

From May 1942 the unit was gradually converted to a bomber squadron. In June the 1st Flight began to receive Pe-2 dive-bombers. The squadron was to operate in the isthmus of Maaselkä area, south-west of the White Sea.

On 30 September 1/LeLv 48 carried out its only Pe-2 sortie of the year by reconnoitring the road system on the isthmus of Maaselkä.

Both photos: PE-212 of 1/LeLv 48 after arriving at Onttola on 4 September 1942. The type was at first used in precision bombing, but this proved to be fruitless and the later duties in photo reconnaissance were much better suited. (SA-kuva)

At the beginning of 1943 the 1st Flight possessed four serviceable Pe-2 aircraft. The unit was tasked with reconnaissance, photography and harassment bombardment.

If the weather permitted 1/LeLv 48 carried out daily reconnaissance and photographing missions with single planes, bombing suitable targets. Harassment bombings were flown against Segesha armament factories and stations on the Murmansk railway.

The bombings ceased at the end of May 1943 after giving no worthwhile results. During the remainder of the year the flight carried out its routine reconnaissance and photographing missions towards Maaselkä.

On 15 November 1943 the squadron was reorganized. Blenheims had arrived as new main equipment for all three flights. Of the serviceable Pe-2s, one remained in the 1st Flight and the other was transferred to the 2nd Flight.

On 28 January 1944 the direction of reconnaissance photography received new orders. First came the Karelian Isthmus, then Olonets Isthmus and last the isthmus of Maaselkä. From March 1944 onwards all Pe-2s flew with the 2nd Flight.

The Pe-2s regularly photographed all air bases in each direction and, based on these pictures, *Lentorykmentti* 4 planned its offensives during the late winter and spring.

From the beginning of June the fast Pe-2s were tasked with photographing the front on the Karelian Isthmus and reconnaissance, carried out through the major offensive beginning on 9 June 1944. Usually four Messerschmitts flew as escort.

On 2 July the 2nd Flight lost two Pe-2s in a Russian air raid on Lappeenranta. The only remaining PE regularly photographed the air bases on the Karelian Isthmus, until 26 July when the last sortie was flown.

S/n	Delivered	Struck off charge	Remarks	Flying Hours
PE-211	10 Jan 1942	9 May 1946	Last flight 4 Apr 1946	264.55
PE-212	10 Jan 1942	17 Jun 1943	W/o Belomorsk 10 Feb 1943	80
PE-213	10 Jan 1942	28 May 1943	W/o Tiiksjärvi 25 Jan 1943	68.10
PE-214	10 Jan 1942	3 Jul 1942	W/o Tampere 21 May 1942	
PE-215	10 Jan 1942	30 Aug 1944	W/o Lappeenranta 2 Jul 1944	173
PE-216	22 Jan 1942	26 Sep 1944	W/o Lake Ladoga 28 Jul 1944	60.15
PE-217	1 Feb 1943	30 Aug 1944	W/o Tali 27 Jun 1944	16.55
PE-301	15 Feb 1941	30 Aug 1944	W/o Lappeenranta 2 Jul 1944	222.10

On 4 September 1944 the cease-fire ended all hostilities between Finland and the Soviet Union. In the Lapland War the solitary Pe-2 carried out one sortie, on 2 October, reconnoitring on route Kemi-Tornio-Rovaniemi and photographing the air base at Kemi.

Pommituslentolaivue 48 flew 125 sorties with the Pe-2 bomber. Four aircraft were lost on operations. A further two were lost in flying accidents or technical failures. Seven aircrew were killed and one became a prisoner of war.

Petlyakov Pe-2 & Pe-3
Camouflage and markings

After refurbishing at the State Aircraft Factory all Pe-2s received the splinter pattern Warpaint of Olive Green and Black with *DN-väri* undersides, keeping these colours through their entire flying career.

PE-213 in air force recognition pictures at Onttola on 26 August 1942. The unit was 1/LeLv 48 and the assigned pilot kapt. *Teuvo Tanskanen. He was killed on 23 January 1943 after running out of fuel on a reconnaissance mission with this plane. (Finnish Air Force)*

PE-213 of 1/LeLv 48 showing its splinter type camouflage pattern in August 1942. (Finnish Air Force)

PE-213 of 1/LeLv 48 at Utti in August 1942, completely in regulation paintwork, including the Black propellers with a 10 cm Yellow blade tip. Special markings consisted of a White bar at the root of one propeller blade. (Pauli Ervi)

Petlyakov Pe-2 in transit markings NS+BA, Malmi airfield, January 1944. Camouflage colours: upper surfaces Dunkelgrün 71, under surfaces Hellblau RLM 65. Markings for captured aircraft Yellow.

Pe-2 coded NS+BA landed at Helsinki Malmi on 29 January 1943. Complying with captured aircraft markings, this particular plane had Yellow cowlings and rudders. Otherwise the camouflage was in RLM colours Dunkelgrün 71 top and Hellblau RLM 65 bottom. This bomber flew with the Finnish Air Force as PE-217. (SA-kuva)

176

Petlyakov Pe-2, PE-213, kapt. Teuvo Tanskanen, flight leader of 1/Lentolaivue 48, Onttola airfield, August 1942. Camouflage colours: upper surfaces Olive Green and Black, under surfaces DN-väri. Standard Eastern Front markings Yellow; serial Olive Green.

PE-213 of 1/LeLv 48 flew to Onttola for official recognition pictures on 26 August 1942. The pilot on this occasion was the flight leader kapt. Aimo Pietarinen. Still in pristine condition after serving in the unit for less than four weeks. (Finnish Air Force)

177

Petlyakov Pe-2, PE-213, kapt. Teuvo Tanskanen, flight leader of 1/Lentolaivue 48, Onttola airfield, August 1942.

PE-213 of 1/LeLv 48 spent most of August 1942 at Utti in training and familiarization. The new type was rather complex with a lot of electric systems. The lack of proper manuals made the task even more difficult. (Pauli Ervi)

Petlyakov Pe-2, PE-213, kapt. Teuvo Tan-skanen, flight leader of 1/Lentolaivue 48, Onttola airfield, August 1942.

179

Petlyakov Pe-2, PE-215, vääp. Aimo Juhola of 1/Lentolaivue 48, Onttola airfield, May 1943. Camouflage colours: upper surfaces Olive Green and Black, under surfaces DN-väri. Standard Eastern Front markings Yellow, serial Olive Green.

PE-215 of 1/LeLv 48 on a visit to Tiiksjärvi in March 1943, flown by the assigned pilot vääp. Aimo Juhola. The regulation Warpaint was applied at the factory on 29 September 1942 though the plane was not delivered to its unit until 2 December 1942. (Kaarlo Temmes)

Petlyakov Pe-2, PE-215, luutn. Kullervo Virtanen of 1/Pommituslentolaivue 48, Onttola airfield, June 1944.

PE-215 of 1/LeLv 48 serviced between missions at Saulajärvi on 9 May 1943. Vääp. Aimo Juhola photographed the front-line at the Karelian Isthmus on this occasion. One blade in each propeller has a white bar, serving as a (friendly marking blinking in flight. (SA-kuva)

Petlyakov Pe-2, PE-211, kapt. Jaakko Ranta, flight leader of 2/Pommituslentolaivue 48, Onttola airfield, August 1944. Camouflage colours: upper surfaces Olive Green and Black, under surfaces DN-väri. Standard Eastern Front markings Yellow, serial Olive Green.

The personnel of 2/PLeLv 48 have gathered around PE-211 at Vesivehmaa in mid-September 1944. The flight leader, kapt. Jaakko Ranta, stands in the cockpit. The tail carries letter A, derived from the squadron CO maj. Esko Ahtiainen. BL-203 in the background has still the yellow markings. (Kullervo Virtanen)

Petlyakov Pe-2, PE-211, kapt. Jaakko Ranta, flight leader of 2/Pommituslento-
laivue 48, Onttola airfield, August 1944.

PE-211 of 2/PLeLv 48 basking in the autumn sun at Vesivehmaa in mid-September 1944. This bomber was
assigned to the flight leader kapt. Jaakko Ranta. This aircraft carries both squadron identifiers, the nose badge
"red devils of Onttola" and tail letter A. The national insignia are of the subdued variety. (Kullervo Virtanen)

183

Junkers Ju 88 A

After the setbacks at Stalingrad and North Africa, the Germans were more willing to sell modern military equipment to its comrade-in-arms Finland. On 12 January 1943 *Reichsmarschall* Hermann Göring promised, on his 50th birthday, that a number of Junkers Ju 88 A-4 bombers would be made available to the Finns. On 24 February the Germans announced that half of the promised 24 aircraft for one squadron could be delivered in February and the rest in March 1943.

The contract was made on 17 April 1943 and the actual deliveries took place on 10, 11 and 20 April 1943. Finnish aircrews flew the planes to Finland, one (JK-274) being lost en route at Riga, Latvia. The serials for the other 23 were JK-251 to JK-273 inclusive, which were applied in Finland, together with the national markings.

Ju 88 A-4 serial JK-252 of 1/LeLv 44 at Onttola on 8 July 1943. The flight identification consisted of a Light Blue-Grey sector on the spinners, separated by a White line from the Black-Green, and RLM 65 outline tail numbers. Otherwise the camouflage was the standard German RLM combination of RLM 70, RLM 71 and RLM 65. (SA-kuva)

JK-252 of 1/LeLv 44 at Onttola on 8 July 1943, photographed from the rear showing the over-painting of the German markings by brush. Small stocks of German colours were obtained for repairing the original paintwork. The fin has a recently applied fighter type tactical number. (SA-kuva)

Continuation War

On 28 April 1943 LeLv 44 commander *ev.luutn.* Birger Gabrielsson brought the first Junkers bomber to the squadron's base at Onttola. The next month was spent in intensive training.

On 30 May LeLv 44 flew the first Junkers mission, when *luutn.* Ahti Nousiainen reconnoitred with JK-261 the railway east from Belomorsk in order to find the Russian transports. Several trains were observed and strafed with machine-gun fire. Three Tomahawks took off from Belomorsk and two chased the Junkers for 20 minutes, firing occasionally.

On 20 August LeR 4 flew a joint bombing mission targeting the Eastern Karelian village of Lehto, where a large partisan supply and training base was located. Thirty-one bombers went to the target assisted by twelve Moranes. The last to enter was LeLv 44 with 16 Junkers led by *ev.luutn.* Gabrielsson, dive-bombing at 04.00–04.15 from 4,000–1,000 m. Six planes scored direct hits on groups of buildings. Two planes dropped bombs while evading fighters. Others dropped bombs in the vicinity of houses.

On 27 August twelve Junkers of LeLv 44 bombed the Pasha river railway bridges south of river Svir, in broad daylight, led by *kapt.* Kosti Lehmus in two patrols. One plane had to return due to engine trouble; one bombed Lake Ladoga by mistake. This was the first use of 1,000 kg bombs in the Finnish Air Force. Hits were scored on the railway embankments but not on the bridges. Six Curtiss fighters covered the return flight.

On 1 September twelve LeLv 44 Junkers led by *kapt.* Erkki Itävuori attacked the Sjassjoki railway bridge, some 50 km south of the mouth of the river Svir. One direct hit was scored in the east end of the bridge and on a flak battery north of the bridge. At the southwest shore of Lake Ladoga the village of Sjasstroi and ships anchored there were strafed with cannon and machine guns. Five Curtiss covered the return over Lake Ladoga.

The evening of 17 September seemed like a good moment for LeR 4 to attack Lavansaari air base, which was to be bombed with 30 planes between 20.15–21.55 and again between 03.00–04.00. Order of attack was LeLv 6, 48, 42, 46 and 44, all from different directions and altitudes. Haze appeared over the Gulf of Finland, causing one hour delay and expectations of a recall, which did not appear.

Last over Lavansaari was LeLv 44. *Kapt.* Lehmus led a 14 plane Junkers formation. the target was hard to see through the thin low cloud over Lavansaari, only flak muzzle flashes assisted in finding the target. The bombing was blind from level flight. No confirmation of hits was obtained, though most bombs did hit the island. On return more haze developed and turned into solid cloud at 100 m. Navigation was extremely hard, resulting in many planes losing their route. Half of the planes found their way back to Utti, where one bellied in. Of the rest, all but one bellied in at different locations.

At 22.55 the second strike was called off. The first one should have been recalled too, but the request by one of the squadron commanders was ignored by the Air Force headquarters.

On 15 November, due to the plane damage incurred by the Lavansaari bombing operation, the 4th Flight of LeLv 44 was disbanded. At the same time, a three-week radio navigation course was initiated for the flying personnel at the Air Force Communications School.

The Soviets had amassed winter depots at the mouth of the river Vodla, at the eastern shore of Lake Onega. LeR 4 was tasked with their destruction, on 29 December.

JK-267 of 2/LeLv 44 about to start a training mission from Onttola on 21 May 1943, with ltm. Unto Oksala at the controls. The dive brakes were removed from the Finnish machines. (Finnish Air Force)

JK-262 of 2/LeLv 44 taking off from Onttola in summer 1943. The regular pilot was the squadron CO, ev.luutn. Birger Gabrielsson. This flight had red spinner tips and red tactical numbers. Typically, most Finnish Ju 88s had the German yellow theatre recognition paint on the underside of the cowlings. (Per Schalin)

Closest to the camera is JK-251 of 1/LeLv 44 at Onttola in summer 1943. The nose shows the flight's new laughing face emblem. Next plane is JK-267 of 3/LeLv 44. (Kari Stenman coll.)

The last operation of the year for LeLv 44 began with *kapt*. Jouko Saarinen leading six Junkers and *luutn*. Tauno Iisalo leading four planes. The formation pushed on in bad weather at 200 m across Lake Onega. The armament was 76x50 kg mines and 32 incendiary torpedoes, with 138 incendiaries in each plane. The first swarm missed the mouth of the Vodla by some 40 km and bombed Kulgala village, starting several fires. The second swarm bombed the target and started many fires.

At the beginning of 1944 *Lentolaivue* 44 possesses seven airworthy Junkers. On 14 February the squadron was renamed as PLeLv 44.

JK-273 of 4/LeLv 44 at Onttola in summer 1943. This flight had a white ring on the spinners and a white outline tail number. The assigned pilot of JK-273 was the flight leader luutn. Tauno Iisalo, who preferred his aircraft without the tactical number. This plane also lacked the yellow underside of the cowlings. (Per Schalin)

JK-270 of 4/LeLv 44 returns from a mission to bomb Lehto partisan base on 20 August 1943. The pilot on this occasion was ltm. Osmo Rantala. Tactical tail number is a white outline 2 (Martti Uotinen)

JK-266 of 3/LeLv 44 at Onttola on 27 August 1943, ready for a mission to bomb the bridges at Pasha river. This was the first occasion when 1,000 kg bombs were dropped. The aircraft was assigned to the flight leader, kapt. Jouko Saarinen. The flight had yellow spinner tips and yellow outline tail numbers, here "1". (Per Schalin)

On 24 February PLeLv 44, led by *ev.luutn.* Gabrielsson, bombed with nine Junkers Russian storage depots by the River Vodla on the eastern shore of Lake Onega. Two large explosions and many fires were seen in the target area.

On 2 March LeR 4 was ordered to bomb Russian airfields on the Karelian Isthmus, with all squadrons. Finnish bombers were to join the returning Russian bomber fleets and bomb the fields, usually well lit, at landing time. Results proved rather good.

On 9 March LeR 4 was given a new chance to infiltrate an ADD bombing mission returning from Tallinn. Over the Gulf of Finland, the Finns joined the formations and flew to their bases. PLeLv 44 joined the Russians west of Kronstadt, with *kapt.* Erkki Itävuori's five Junkers bombing Kasimovo from 1,600 m at 21.30–21.35, hitting the runway and rows of planes, causing one immediate explosion and two fires. After the exit, a large explosion and many fires seen.

On 3 April LeR 4 concentrated 34 planes for an attack on the airfield at Kähy, north-east of Leningrad. Aerial reconnaissance had found 57 planes there the day before. First to bomb was PLeLv 44, led by *kapt*. Itävuori's nine Junkers. Hits were recorded on target, three large and three smaller fires lit. One bomb caused an explosion.

After the spring thaw was over, the airfield of Mergino at the mouth of the River Svir became a target once more. On 19 May LeR 4 took off with 42 planes. Forty-one planes bombed the base right after midnight. This was the biggest number of planes the regiment ever managed to get to the target. PLeLv 44 led off with *kapt*. Lehmus and his eight Junkers, hitting the target area. No accurate assessment of hits could be made due to dusk and heavy haze.

After the success achieved against Germany in the spring of 1944, the Soviet Union began in the Karelian Isthmus the fourth of ten strategic efforts; this was to be the only one which did not reach

JK-265 of 3/LeLv 44 ready for a training mission from Onttola on 3 October 1943. The bombs are 250 kg drill items and on this occasion the pilot was the flight leader, kapt. *Jouko Saarinen. This machine was equipped with the 20 mm nose cannon, operated by the observer. In Finnish bomber crews the observer was the plane captain. (SA-kuva)*

JK-265 of 3/LeLv 44 at Onttola in summer 1943. The regular pilot was ltm. Unto Oksala. Tactical number is a yellow outline 4. (Kari Stenman coll.)

JK-258 of 2/LeLv 44 at Onttola just before a landing accident on 17 May 1943. It was repaired in three months. (Kari Stenman coll.)

JK-252 of 1/LeLv 44 at Onttola in May 1943, before the application of the flight badge to the nose. (Kari Stenman coll.)

its goals. The offensive started on 9 June, and on the next day the first Finnish line of defence was breached, forcing the Finns to retreat.

On 9 June LeR 4 was given an order to prepare for an all-out attack in the Karelian Isthmus. To avoid losses and spare the sparse resources, the regiment ordered attacks to take place primarily at night. Russian breakthroughs forced the air forces to act without regard to losses.

On 12 June LeR 4 performed its first combined bombing at the blocking battles being fought in the Karelian Isthmus. The 38 planes, including 14 PLeLv 44 Junkers, had tanks and columns on the Kivennapa-Mainila road as targets.

On 14 June in the evening, a few hours before a counter attack by a Finnish tank division, LeR 4 attacked Russian tank forces seen on the open areas of Kuuterselkä with a total of 33 planes. PLeLv 44 sent eleven Junkers on a dive bombing mission led by *kapt*. Itävuori, dive-bombing the tank formations at Kuuterselkä. Five Airacobra fighters met the bombers over the target. One Junkers was hit in the wing, and one was rescued by friendly Messerschmitt escort fighters attacking the Russians.

Next day PLeLv 44 supported the fight with 11 Junkers and assisted a counter attack by dive-bombing Russian tanks and rocket launchers on the plains of Siiranmäki, escorted by eight Messerschmitts

On 16 June LeR 4 targeted a naval convoy of 36 ships south of Koivisto, heading west-north-west. Six large ships were part of the convoy. The regiment sent 30 planes to attack at 15.39, and caused the convoy to disperse and lay a smokescreen. This did not impede bombing, which was performed in small groups and single planes within fifteen minutes. PLeLv 44 dive-bombed last with *kapt*. Lehmus and his ten Junkers, hitting one rather large ship hit with two bombs and two fell right by it; direct hits on two other ships were seen and one of them went out of view. Due to the smokescreen one plane was unable to observe the bombing, but 15 seconds later a black column of smoke arose from the screen.

On 19 June just before midnight, LeR 4 took off with 35 planes to attack the Humaljoki estuary, where an amphibious enemy fleet was approaching. Dusk made it impossible for some planes to see the ships, and eight planes bombed secondary targets on the coast. The bombs dropped on the convoy fell in the middle of the ships, and flak of some ships ceased to fire. Other than that, no appraisal of hits was possible.

LeR 4 could initially afford only one attack on the eastern coast of Lake Ladoga. An amphibious enemy fleet was hit with 17 planes on 23 June. PLeLv 44 sent *kapt*. Saarinen and his 11 Junkers to dive-bomb the target at 04.45–04.52. A direct hit was gained on one large vessel and it sank,

JK-252 of 1/LeLv 44 at Onttola in summer 1943, frequently flown by the flight leader kapt. *Erkki Itävuori. He also painted the flight emblem onto the back of his leather jacket. (Kari Stenman coll.)*

other bombs fell close to the vessels. One more ship was seen to sink and two were in flames when the planes left the target.

As PLeLv 44 dive-bombed in the evening on 28 June the bridges of Tali and Russian artillery positions nearby, led by *maj*. Tauno Meller, the Russians had already advanced out of the narrow terrain of Tali and around Leitimojärvi on both sides towards Portinhoikka and Ihantalanjärvi. After the bombing it was seen that one stick of bombs hit the bridge. A flight of Messerschmitts flew top cover.

In the afternoon on 29 June, PLeLv 44 attacked the bridges of Saarela Manor west of Tali, where the Russians were about to enter the crossroads at Portinhoikka. *Maj.* Meller led 12 Junkers to dive-bomb the bridges, of which one was cut. An escort of eight Messerschmitts flew alongside the bombers.

On 30 June LeR 4 sent 40 planes to bomb enemy groupings, vehicles, and tanks at the Portinhoikka area of Ihantala. There were 19 Messerschmitts flying escort, and this 59 plane detachment was the biggest ever Finnish formation during the entire war.

Russian assault forces landed at the Bay of Viipuri to attack Finnish forces, hitting Teikarinsaari first on 1 July. PLeLv 44 sent seven Junkers of *kapt*. Saarinen to bomb landing vessels at the coast at Pulliniemi. Dive-bombing led to one direct hit on a big vessel which exploded and disappeared.

JK-273 of 2/LeLv 44 at Onttola in early 1944, assigned to luutn. *Tauno Iisalo, acting now as the flight deputy leader. The squadron was re-organized on 15 November by cutting the number of flights from four to three. Iisalo was a prominent bomber pilot and one of only four decorated with the Mannerheim Cross. (Martti Perälä)*

Two bombs hit the bow of another big ship. An explosion was seen in the ship and it stopped in flames. A small ship in front of the ship sank right away. A 1000 kg bomb hit some 15 m away from a big ship which stopped and emitted a large black oil slick.

On 4 July early in the morning, LeR 4 bombed a naval convoy with 37 planes while the convoy moved under cover of smoke at Tuppuransaari. Two direct hits on ships were obtained and there was also a forceful explosion seen in the middle of the artificial smoke, out of which a high column of smoke arose.

On 5 July the Russian advance at Tali and Ihantala stalled because of ferocious defence by the Finns. Now it was time for the last but one all-regiment bombing mission to Tali. Thirty-six planes took off to bomb artillery positions.

LeR 4 initiated focused attacks against the river crossing preparations at Vuosalmi. At 8 pm an attack by 34 planes was carried out, targeting tanks and artillery at Äyräpää. The bombs hit concentrated Russian forces. A big explosion was seen and many fires were lit.

On 7 July in the morning PLeLv 44 sent nine Junkers to dive-bomb Russian ships at Uuras, 25 ships were counted. Two big ships were hit and one of them sank. Many near misses were also obtained and as the planes left the target area, three ships were burning. Nine Messerschmitts flew top cover.

Six aircraft under kapt. Erkki Itävuori were flown to Utti, from where they attacked Leningrad area air bases, by joining the returning Soviet bombers and releasing the bombs when they landed on fully lit airfields on 9 March 1944. The nearest bomber is JK-255. (Martti Perälä)

The bombings of Äyräpää and Vuosalmi were the peak of LeR 4 activities in the summer of 1944, as it was attempted to stem Russian operations by focused bombing attacks. The regiment flew to targets at Äyräpää and Vuosalmi twelve times, with an average strength of 30 planes, with no losses despite furious Russian flak and plenty of fighter activity.

On the morning of 8 July the targets were tanks, infantry groups, and artillery positions at Äyräpää. Thirty-one bombers were escorted by eleven MTs. PLeLv 44 was the first to arrive with *kapt.* Erkki Itävuori and his nine Junkers, dive-bombing the target at 6 am. Six planes hit the target area and three more hit the immediate vicinity.

On 9 July the Russians began crossing Vuosalmi south of Paakkola, despite heavy losses. In broad daylight LeR 4 attacked with 33 bombers, escorted by eight Messerschmitts. The bombs struck the river crossing at Äyräpää and many explosions were seen at the target.

On 14 July LeR 4 went out on full force attacks three times, early in the morning with 43 bombers to Käsnäselkä on the north-east shores of Lake Ladoga, then later in the day to Äyräpää also with 33 planes, and in the evening to Pitkäranta on the northeast side of Lake Ladoga with 32 aircraft.

On 15 July the war entered a stationary phase all over the Karelian Isthmus, as Russian troops dug in for defence. LeR 4 flew regimental bombing efforts three times once more. Early in the morning the target for 32 planes was the river crossing at Äyräpää, at noon there was a 26 plane attack on artillery positions at Nietjärvi behind Lake Ladoga, and in the evening another attack by 27 planes flew to bomb the Vuosalmi bridgehead. Two flights of Messerschmitts escorted the planes over the Isthmus, and on the Nietjärvi mission a flight of Brewsters and Curtiss flew top cover.

By 18 July the Russian attacks had subsided at Vuosalmi, having managed to make a breach to the north of the River Vuoksi, some five kilometres wide and two kilometres deep. The morning regimental bombing of Vuosalmi was decided to be executed at an altitude a couple kilometres higher than usual. Thirty bombers and 16 Messerschmitts took off to carry out the mission. PLeLv 44 rounded off the mission with *kapt.* Erkki Itävuori and his eight Junkers, this time by horizontal bombing from 4,400 m and hitting the target area.

On 22 July early in the morning LeR 4 bombed with 34 planes, including nine Junkers, the troops and artillery positions between Lake Vegarus and Lake Kollaa. A sizeable explosion was seen at the target. Five Moranes escorted the bombers.

JK-267 of 3/PLeLv 44 during an overhaul at Luonetjärvi. On 1 April 1944 vääp. *Tauno Kaarma flew it back to Onttola. The bars hanging from the ventral hatch are the ladder.*

On 28 July early in the morning LeR 4 sent 30 planes to bomb artillery positions in the Kollaanjärvi-Näätäoja area. The new commander of PLeLv 44, *maj.* Tauno Meller, led seven JKs to bomb tanks at Korpijärvi. Many small explosions were seen and one large one, too. Twelve Curtiss and Moranes flew escort.

On 9 August PLeLv 44 had its final war mission when the last regimental bombing effort was sent to attack Suojärvi station with 30 planes. The goal was to disrupt the retreat of moving equipment. The planes went in two waves, escorted by six Messerschmitts. Ahead of the others was PLeLv 44 and *luutn.* Eero Joutsen's eight Junkers, dive-bombing the assigned target at 20.34 from 4,000 to 2,500 m. Hits were observed on the rail yard, a storage house was blown up, two fires were seen. Incendiaries fell short of the target and went into the forest.

JK-254 of 1/PLeLv 44 received two 40 mm flak hits in the tail on 12 June 1944, when piloted by ltm. Martti Perälä. The aircraft was repaired in six days, only to be lost in a flying accident on 1 July 1944. The tactical number is a Light Blue-Grey outline 3. (SA-kuva)

JK-256 of 1/PLeLv 44 assigned to the flight leader kapt. Erkki Itävuori, seen here bombed up at Onttola in mid-June 1944. The 250 kg and 500 kg bombs have been decorated with skulls and crossbones. Appropriate to the boss, the tactical number is a Light Blue-grey outline 1. (SA-kuva)

In the Continuation War PLeLv 44 flew 558 sorties with the Ju 88, one was shot down by a fighter and seven were lost in flying accidents, killing twelve airmen.

On 4 September 1944 the commander of the Air Force ordered the air regiments to tell squadrons to cease fighting at 7.00. A ceasefire commenced and two weeks later it was confirmed by The Moscow Armistice.

LAPLAND WAR

On 4 September the Air Force set up the Special Staff Sarko, with *ev.* Olavi Sarko commanding, to conduct the air war in Lapland, subordinating to him LeR 2 and LeR 4, which were ordered to prepare to participate in the war.

The III Army Corps, formed in Lapland, had started its attack three days earlier, but real action only began when the Finns made a surprise landing in the rear of the Germans in Tornio on October 1.

The first offensive mission of LeR 4 was to bomb on 2 October German troops, vehicles and columns, which were retreating along the main roads to Rovaniemi. Squadrons took off at intervals from their bases some 500 km away. PLeLv 44 came in with *maj.* Tauno Meller's ten Junkers at 15.40–16.47 to bomb columns between Kemi and Rovaniemi and again on the Ranua-Rovaniemi road.

All bombings were at less than 1,000 m altitude, and the Finns reported many direct hits on columns, but the Germans considered the damage minimal. On the whole, the Northern bombing offensive remained at nuisance level, because the German radar-controlled and very intense flak shot through clouds and forced bombing altitudes to be elevated, which in turn reduced accuracy.

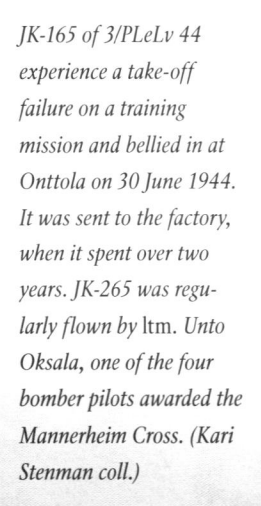

JK-165 of 3/PLeLv 44 experience a take-off failure on a training mission and bellied in at Onttola on 30 June 1944. It was sent to the factory, when it spent over two years. JK-265 was regularly flown by ltm. Unto Oksala, one of the four bomber pilots awarded the Mannerheim Cross. (Kari Stenman coll.)

On 6 October PLeLv 44 possessed eleven Junkers in two flights. Six Junkers bombers attacked the Aapajoki railroad and vehicle bridges north of Tornio, led by *kapt*. Saarinen, but while they hit the railroad, the bridges remained intact.

On 8 October LeR 4 sent all its squadrons to bomb the Germans retreating from Tornio and Kemi towards Rovaniemi. PLeLv 44 attacked twice, with six Junkers, the columns of German troops and vehicles retreating to Rovaniemi. The crowded columns were hit badly. Brewsters flew as escort.

On 10 October LeR 4 bombed German troops with 23 planes along the road between Rovaniemi and Ranua. The six PLeLv 44 Junkers were led by *maj*. Meller. Direct hits were seen among troops and on the roads. A hit was scored on the bridge across the river flowing from Perunkajärvi. At least four Bf 109Gs attacked the formation and fired on many planes, shooting one down.

On 22 October three Junkers of PLeLv 44, led by *kapt*. Saarinen, bombed a column of trucks on the road at Jerisjärvi between Kittilä and Muonio.

S/n	C/n	Delivered	Struck off charge	Remarks	Flying Hours
JK-251	088 3880	10 Apr 1943	15 Feb 1944	W/o Onttola 29 Dec 1943	62.55
JK-252	088 3878	10 Apr 1943	1 Oct 1952	Into storage 15 Sep 1948	200+
JK-253	088 3879	10 Apr 1943	1 Oct 1952	W/o Luonetjärvi 26 Aug 1947	213.40
JK-254	088 3883	10 Apr 1943	12 Aug 1944	W/o Liperi 1 July 1944	119.10
JK-255	088 3889	10 Apr 1943	26 Jul 1944	W/o Utti 6 Jun 1944	98.40
JK-256	088 3860	20 Apr 1943	12 Dec 1944	W/o Simo 10 Oct 1944	210.50
JK-257	088 3887	20 Apr 1943	1 Oct 1952	Into storage 15 Sep 1948	100+
JK-258	088 8797	20 Apr 1943	1 Oct 1952	Into storage 15 Sep 1948	150+
JK-259	088 3845	20 Apr 1943	26 Jul 1944	W/o Salmi 23 Jun 1944	112.20
JK-260	088 8785	20 Apr 1943	20 Feb 1945	W/o S of Leningrad 6 Oct 1944	159.45
JK-261	088 3857	20 Apr 1943	29 Jul 1947	W/o Kemi 5 Jun 1946	50+
JK-262	088 3899	11 Apr 1943	9 Oct 1944	W/o Mensuvaara 18 Jul 1944	192.30
JK-263	088 3863	11 Apr 1943	2 Feb 1945	W/o Rovaniemi 15 Oct 1944	84.55
JK-264	088 8794	20 Apr 1943	31 Jul 1944	W/o Kesälahti 15 Jun 1944	58.50
JK-265	088 3877	10 Apr 1943	1 Oct 1952	Into storage 15 Sep 1948	200+
JK-266	088 3885	10 Apr 1943	11 Dec 1952	Last flight 15 Oct 1945	195
JK-267	088 3888	11 Apr 1943	11 Dec 1952	W/o Onttola 29 Jul 1944	140.05
JK-268	088 8796	20 Apr 1943	1 Oct 1952	Into storage 15 Sep 1948	150+
JK-269	088 3882	10 Apr 1943	11 Dec 1952	W/o Onttola 20 Aug 1943	46.35
JK-270	088 3881	10 Apr 1943	1 Oct 1952	Into storage 15 Sep 1948	200+
JK-271	088 3841	20 Apr 1943	1 Oct 1952	Into storage 15 Sep 1948	200+
JK-272	088 8795	20 Apr 1943	22 Jun 1950	W/o Luonetjärvi 22 Feb 1947	269.45
JK-273	088 3912	20 Apr 1943	28 Jul 1947	W/o Laukaa 18 Jun 1947	383.55
JK-274	088 3849	20 Apr 1943		W/o Riga, Latvia 23 Apr 1943	6.35

By October 28, the initial 41 bomber strength of LeR 4 had fallen down to 23 operational planes. Next operation was on 16 November, when three Junkers bombed a German storage area at Suikero and one plane attacked a vehicle convoy north of Naimakkajärvi.

On 4 December 1944 the Air Force was returned to its peacetime strength. The squadrons were renumbered, PLeLv 44 becoming PLeLv 43. The strength was down to six Junkers and reconnaissance and harassment bombings continued, when weather permitted.

On December 21, two bomber pilots were awarded the Mannerheim Cross. They were *kapt.*Tauno Iisalo of PLeLv 44 and *luutn.* Lauri Äijö, an observer of the same squadron. They were the last knights of the Air Force.

The Finnish troops reached the Kilpisjärvi falls on 12 January 1945. This was to be the final war zone until April 27, when the last Germans retreated over the border to Norway.

PLeLv 43 continued reconnaissance with single aircraft and harassment bombings by two or three Junker, until 4 April 1945, when JK-268 left for the last mission of the type in this war and flew out to the Arctic Sea fjords, returning to Kemi at 4 pm.

The Lapland War lasted for 183 days, on only 43 of which was the weather was good enough for flying. LeR 4 took off on 516 sorties, of which 111 had to be recalled due to weather. The Junkers of PLeLv 44/43 flew 116 sorties, losing three aircraft and nine members of the aircrew.

Junkers Ju 88 A
Camouflage and markings

On arrival in Finland the Ju 88 were in standard German bomber camouflage, upper sides in RLM dark green colours *Schwartzgrün* RLM 70 and *Dunkelgrün* 71 with *Hellblau* RLM 65 undersides. The German markings were often crudely painted over and Finnish insignias and serials were applied at the air depot.

These colours existed until the next major repair. The first one to have applied Warpaint of Olive Green and Black was JK-260 on 25 April 1944, followed by JK-268 a fortnight later. In June 1944 JK-264, 271, 272 and 253 received Warpaint and JK-263 and 252 by the end of the year. These camouflage colours were retained until the end of their flying career in September 1948.

JK-260 of 2/PLeLv 44 taking off from Onttola on 14 July 1944, with the regular pilot ltm. Osmo Rantala at the controls. The aircraft has the proper flight colour spinners already fitted, though the port one appears to have a black tip. (SA-kuva)

JK-258 of 2/PLeLv 44 seen in flight during the summer 1944 campaign. The regular pilot was luutn. *Ahti Nousiainen, one of very few bomber pilots to fly over 100 missions. The aircraft lacks the tactical tail number. (Per Schalin)*

JK-268 of 3/PLeLv 44 returns to Onttola from a mission to Kuuterselkä on 14 June 1944. The pilot on this occasion was luutn. Kalevi Heiskanen. Tail number is a yellow outline 5. (SA-kuva)

The laughing face emblem of 1/PLeLv 44 was painted also on the back of the flight leader kapt Erkki Itävuori's leather jacket. Here a truck is taking the air crews to their planes at Onttola in mid-June 1944. (SA-kuva)

JK-255 of 1/PLeLv 44 suffered a take-off accident at Utti on 1 June 1944, becoming a write-off. All three flight identifiers can be seen, spinners, nose badge and tail number. Also note the crude over-painting of the German wing Balkenkreutz. (Finnish Air Force)

Junkers Ju 88 A-4, BJ+WW (JK-271) in ferry markings, Pori airfield, April 1943. Camouflage colours: upper surfaces Schwartzgrün 70 and Dunkelgrün 71, under surfaces Hellblau 65. Standard Eastern Front markings Yellow.

Ju 88 A-4 with Stammkennzeichen BJ+WW seen at Pori, where the aircraft arrived on 23 April 1943. The German markings were over-painted and the Finnish serial JK-271 applied, before handing over to 4/LeLv 44 on 8 May 1943. (Kari Stenman coll.)

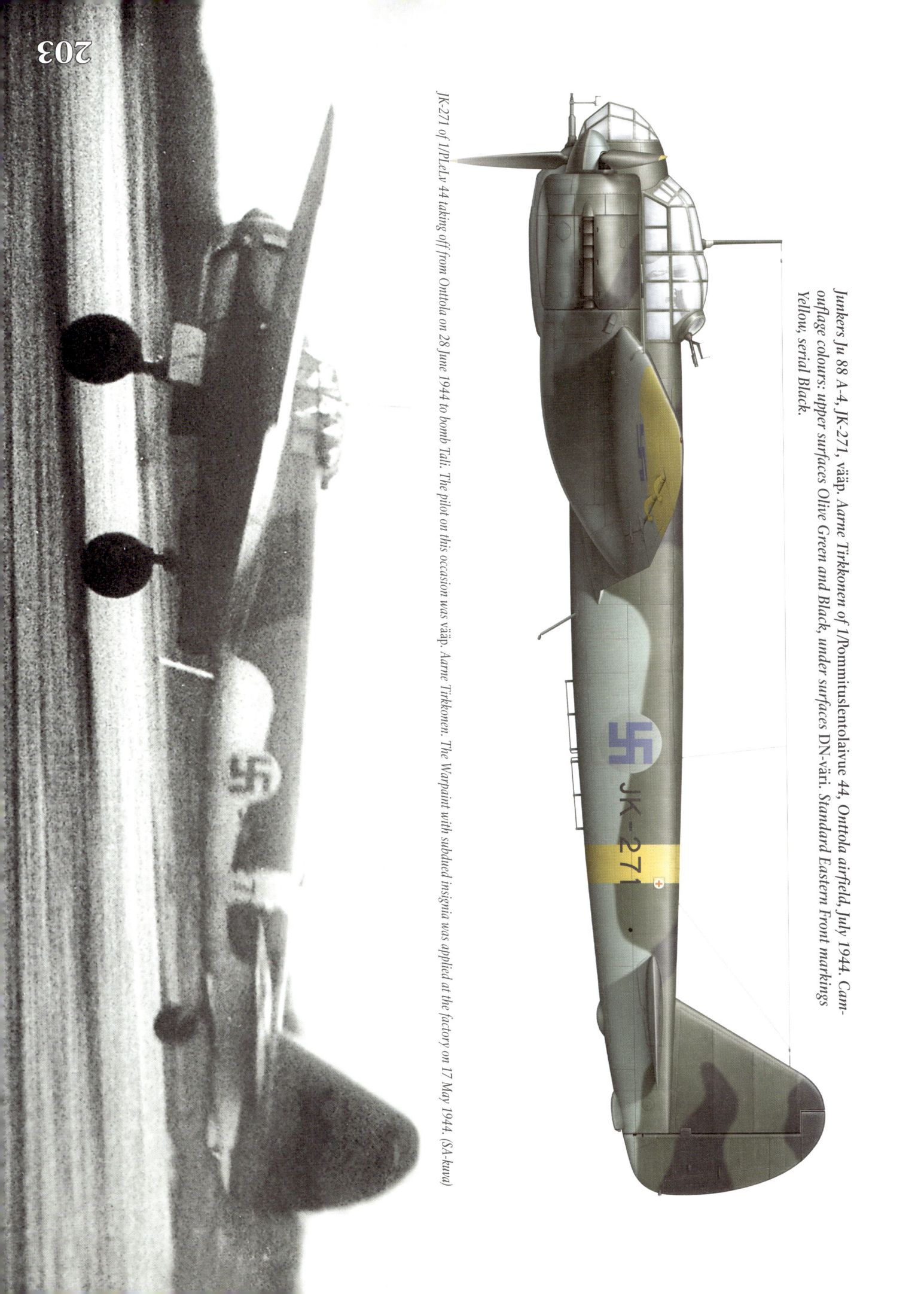

Junkers Ju 88 A-4, JK-271, vääp. Aarne Tirkkonen of 1/Pommituslentolaivue 44, Onttola airfield, July 1944. Camouflage colours: upper surfaces Olive Green and Black, under surfaces DN-väri. Standard Eastern Front markings Yellow, serial Black.

JK-271 of 1/PLeLv 44 taking off from Onttola on 28 June 1944 to bomb Tali. The pilot on this occasion was vääp. Aarne Tirkkonen. The Warpaint with subdued insignia was applied at the factory on 17 May 1944. (SA-kuva)

Junkers Ju 88 A-4, JK-267, ltm. Osmo Metsola, 3/Lentolaivue 44, Onttola airfield, August 1943. Camouflage colours: upper surfaces Schwartzgrün 70 and Dunkelgrün 71, under surfaces Hellblau 65. Standard Eastern Front markings Yellow, serial White.

JK-267 of 3/LeLv 44 showing the standard German upper surface camouflage pattern of RLM greens 70 and 71. It is flying here over a lake near Onttola on 21 May 1943. (Finnish Air Force)

JK-267 of 3/PLeLv 44 at Luonetjärvi on 1 April 1944. It was regularly flown by ltm. Osmo Metsola. until 29 July 1944 when crashed at take-off due to engine failure. (SA-kuva)

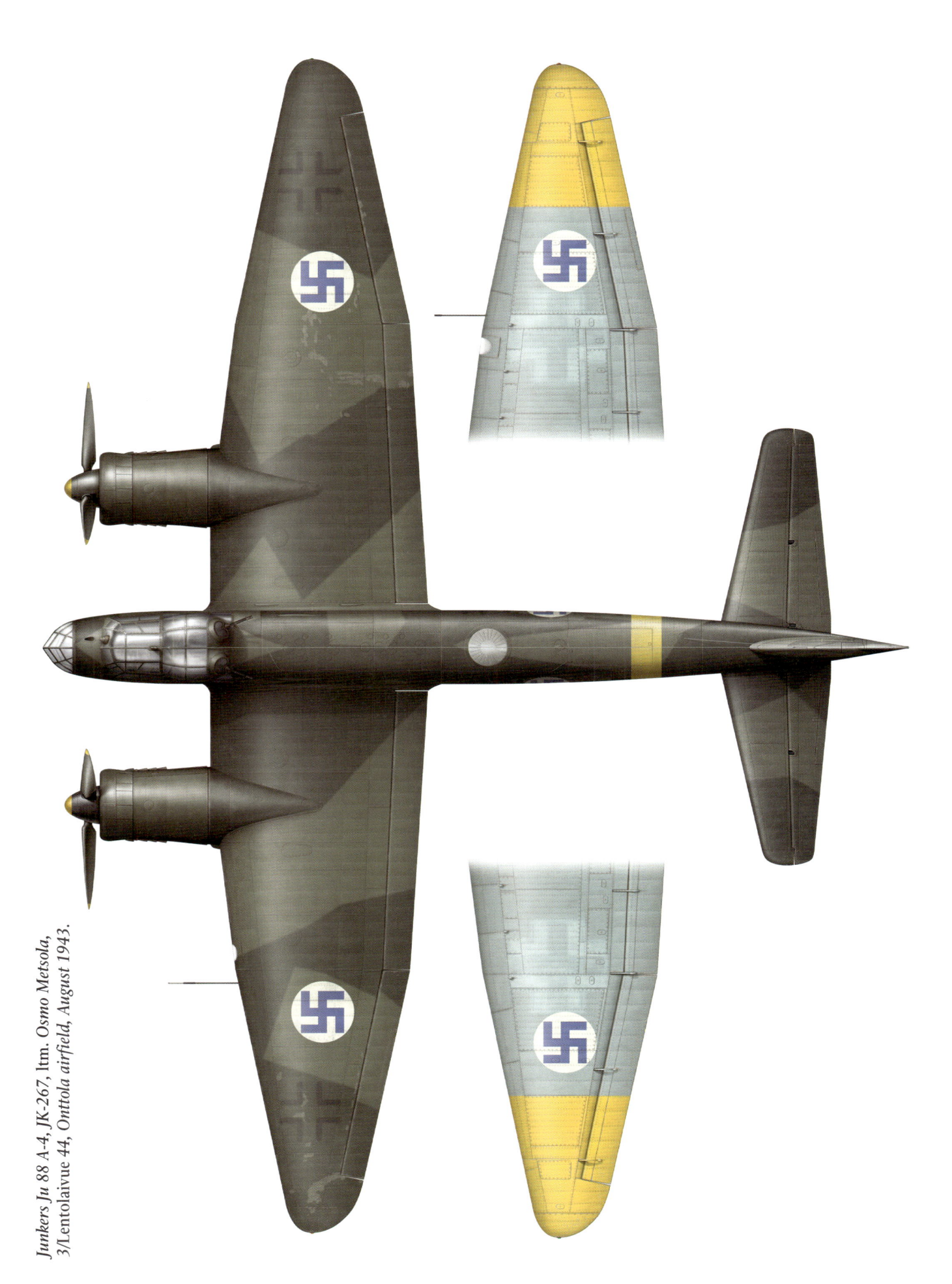

Junkers Ju 88 A-4, JK-267, ltm. Osmo Metsola,
3/Lentolaivue 44, Onttola airfield, August 1943.

Junkers Ju 88 A-4, JK-267, ltm. Osmo Metsola, 3/Lentolaivue 44, Onttola airfield, August 1943.

JK-267 of 3/LeLv 44 taking off from Onttola, before a belly landing on 9 September 1943. The repair took 3½ months. The flight identifiers were yellow propeller spinner tips and yellow outline tail number, here 3. (Martti Perälä)

Junkers Ju 88 A-4, JK-255, ltm. Martti Perälä, 1/Pommituslentolaivue 44, Onttola airfield, March 1944. Camouflage colours: upper surfaces Schwartzgrün 70 and Dunkelgrün 71, under surfaces Hellblau 65. Standard Eastern Front markings Yellow, serial White.

JK-255 of 1/PLeLv 44 at Onttola in early 1944. It was regularly flown by ltm. Martti Perälä. Tactical tail number Light Blue-Grey 5 shows to good advantage. The over-paint of the German wing insignia was done with fresh paint. (Martti Perälä)

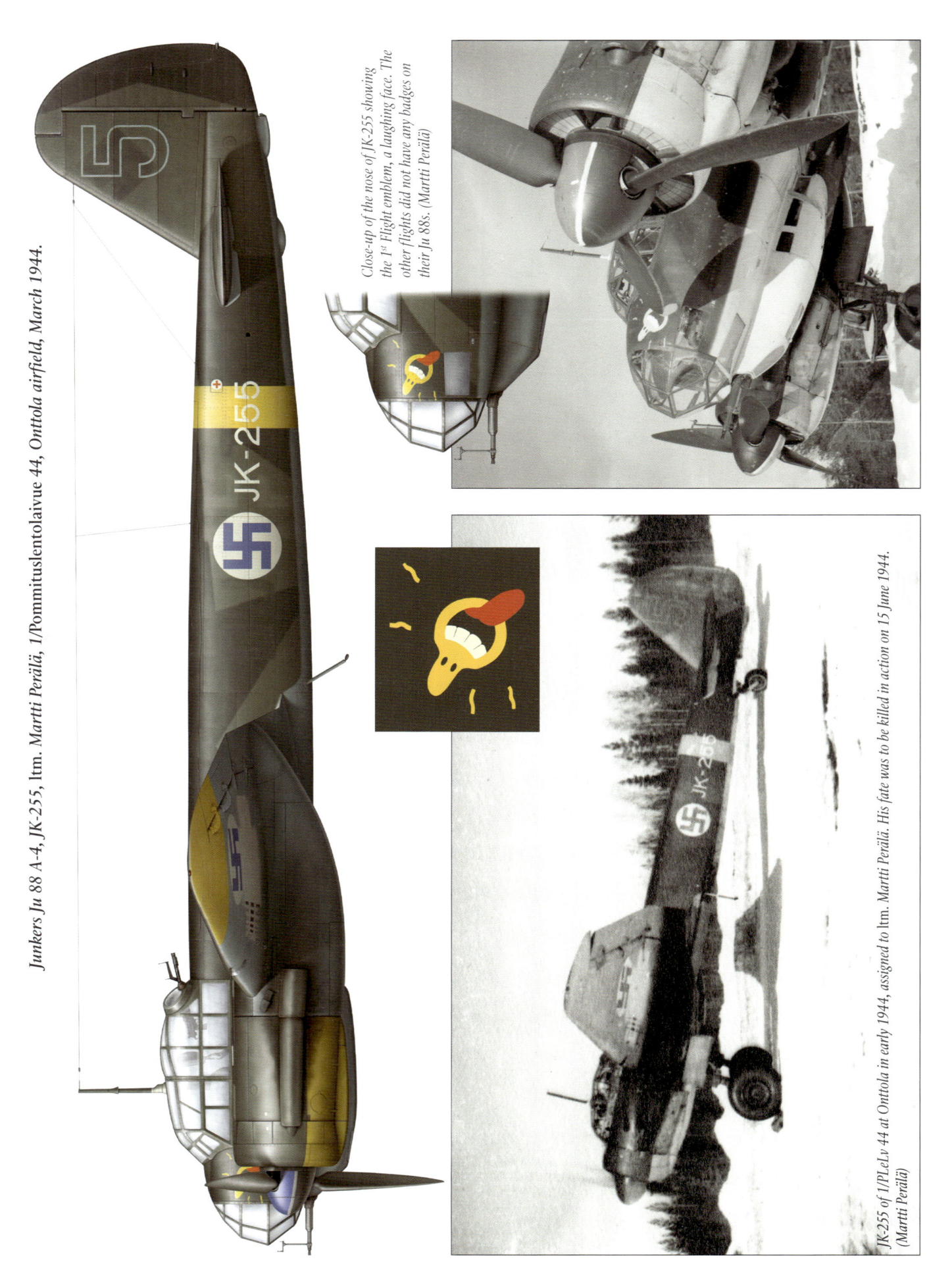

Junkers Ju 88 A-4, JK-255, ltm. Martti Perälä, 1/Pommituslentolaivue 44, Onttola airfield, March 1944.

Close-up of the nose of JK-255 showing the 1st Flight emblem, a laughing face. The other flights did not have any badges on their Ju 88s. (Martti Perälä)

JK-255 of 1/PLeLv 44 at Onttola in early 1944, assigned to ltm. Martti Perälä. His fate was to be killed in action on 15 June 1944. (Martti Perälä)

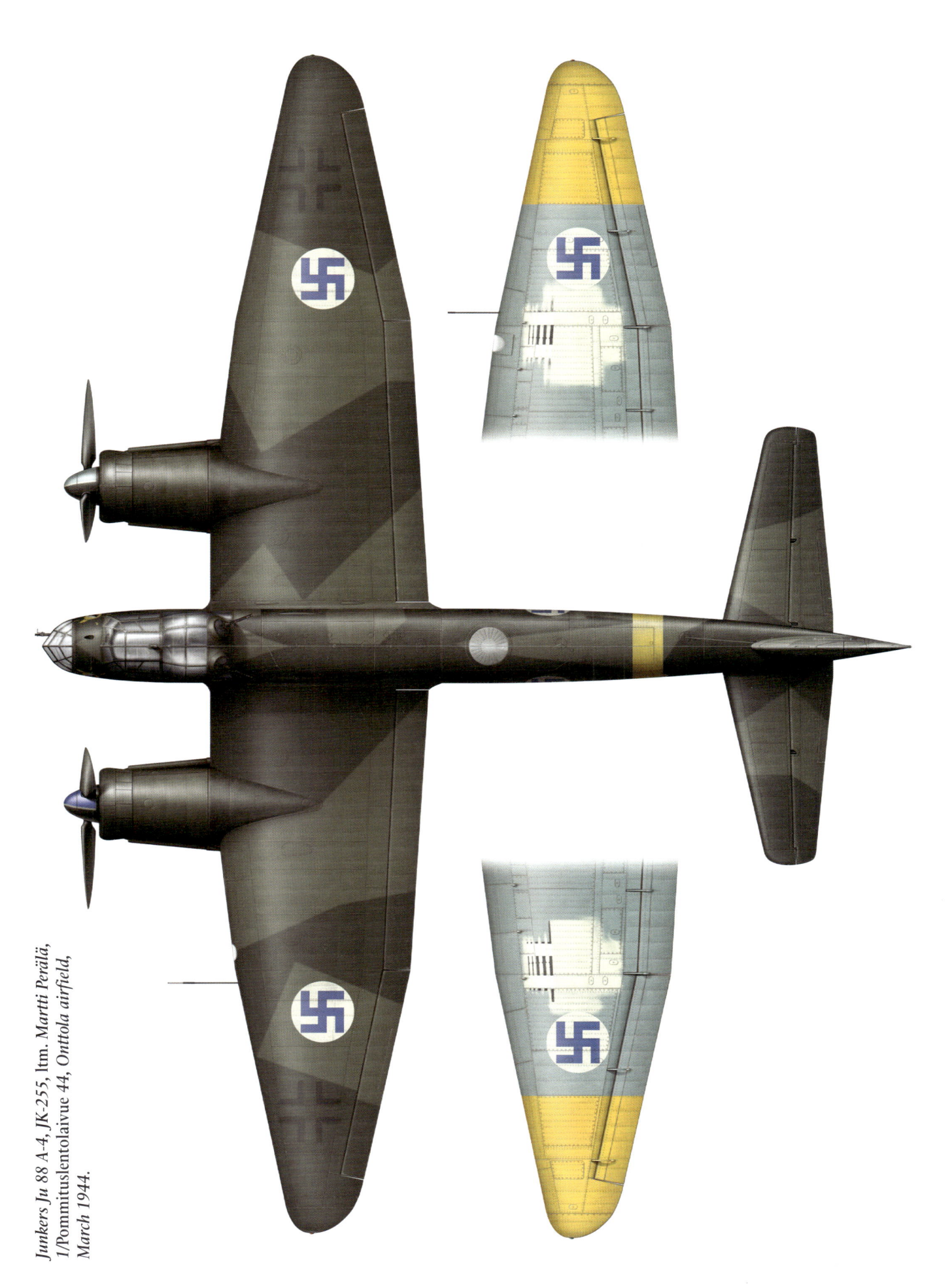

*Junkers Ju 88 A-4, JK-255, ltm. Martti Perälä,
1/Pommituslentolaivue 44, Onttola airfield,
March 1944.*

209

Junkers Ju 88 A-4, JK-262, ev.luutn. Birger Gabrielsson, CO of Lentolaivue 44 in 2/Lentolaivue 44 markings, Onttola airfield, August 1943. Camouflage colours: upper surfaces Schwartzgrün 70 and Dunkelgrün 71, under surfaces Hellblau 65. Standard Eastern Front markings Yellow, serial White.

JK-262 of 2/LeLv 44 being bombed up at Onttola in June 1943. The aircraft was regularly flown by the squadron CO ev. luutn. Birger Gabrielsson. The 2nd Flight had Red spinner tips and Red tail numbers, here 3. (Kari Stenman coll.)

Junkers Ju 88 A-4, JK-272, ylik. Mikko Nikula, 4/Lentolaivue 44, Onttola airfield, August 1943. Camouflage colours: upper surfaces Schwartzgrün 70 and Dunkelgrün 71, under surfaces Hellblau 65. Standard Eastern Front markings Yellow, serial White.

JK-272 of 4/LeLv 44 during an overhaul parked near the hangar at Luonetjärvi. On 25 August the regular pilot ylik. Mikko Nikula flew the plane back to Onttola. This flight had a white ring on the propeller spinners and white outline tail number. (Kari Stenman coll.)

Junkers Ju 88 A-4, JK-260, ltm. Osmo Rantala, 2/Pommituslentolaivue 44, Onttola airfield, July 1944. Camou-flage colours: upper surfaces Olive Green and Black, under surfaces DN-väri. Standard Eastern Front markings Yellow, serial Black.

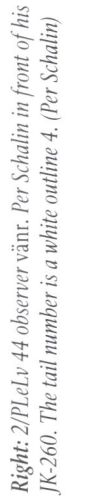

Below: 2/PLeLv 44 leader and future Mannerheim Cross winner luutn. Tauno Iisalo in front of JK-260. (Per Schalin)

Right: 2/PLeLv 44 observer vänr. Per Schalin in front of his JK-260. The tail number is a white outline 4. (Per Schalin)

Left: JK-260 of 2/PLeLv 44 taking off from Onttola in the latter half of June 1944, assigned to ltm. Osmo Rantala. The spinners are still in 1st Flight colours. (SA-kuva)

212

Junkers Ju 88 A-4, JK-260, ltm. Osmo Rantala, 2/Pommituslentolaivue 44, Onttola airfield, July 1944.

Junkers Ju 88 A-4, JK-260, ltn. Osmo Rantala, 2/Pommituslentolaivue 44, Onttola airfield, July 1944.

JK-260 of 2/PLeLv 44 about to take off for a mission from Onttola in mid-June 1944, carrying one 1,000 kg and two 250 kg bombs. This particular machine was the first to receive the Warpaint on 1 March 1944, with subdued national insignia. (SA-kuva)

Junkers Ju 88 A-4, JK-268, luutn. Kalevi Heiskanen, 3/Pommituslentolaivue 44, Onttola airfield, June 1944. Camouflage colours: upper surfaces Olive Green and Black, under surfaces DN-väri. Standard Eastern Front markings Yellow, serial Black.

JK-268 of 3/PLeLv 44 returns to Onttola from a mission to Kuuterselkä on 14 June 1944. The pilot on this occasion was luutn. Kalevi Heiskanen. Tail number is a Yellow outline 5. The Warpaint was factory applied on 21 March 1944. (SA-kuva)

Appendices

Bomber camouflage and markings

When a standard camouflage was introduced in 1933, it consisted of *Kenttävihreä* (Olive Green) upper surfaces and aluminium lacquer lower surfaces. This concerned all aircraft whether locally built or imported, the exception being four Dutch-built Fokker C.X light bombers, where the Olive Green was replaced by original *Camouflage Bruin*.

From 20 March 1934 the national insignia size was defined as 4/5th of the wing chord, but on 23 July 1940 the maximum size was limited to 100 cm.

The Warpaint scheme was issued on 30 September 1940, by adding broad black stripes, in proportion of 2:3 in favour of the Olive Green as specified on 1 November 1940. This upper surface scheme was valid until the storage of all bombers in September 1948.

During the mobilization for the Continuation War, all Finnish aircraft received Yellow theatre markings, a 50 cm wide band around the rear fuselage and wing tip undersides to 1/6th of the span. These markings were removed after the armistice on 4 September 1944.

When the German Do 17 Zs arrived in January 1942, their *Hellblau* (RLM 65) lower colour was tested on BL-129 from 19 March 1942. This led to an order on 7 May 1942 to paint the lower surfaces of all warplanes in *DN-väri* (RLM 65), carried out at the next repair or major overhaul.

On 12 January 1944 an order was given to subdue the white circle of the national insignia with *DN-väri* (factory) or Light Grey (units), to be done in the next repair or overhaul. The swastika insignia was replaced by a Blue and White cockade from 1 April 1945.

Table with the types of colours identified by codes

Origin	Colour description	FS equivalent	Used on
Finnish	Kenttävihreä / Olive Green	34096	BL, LY, FK, DC, DB, DF, SB,PE, DN, JK
Finnish	Hopeanharmaa / Aluminium dope	17178	All but DN, PE, DF, JK
Finnish	Vaalen Harmaa / Light Grey	16440	FK
Finnish	Musta / Black	37038	BL, LY, FK, DC, DB, DF, SB,PE, DN, JK
Finnish	Keltainen / Rich Yellow	13538	BL, LY, FK, DC, DB, DF, SB,PE, DN, JK
Finnish	Keltainen / Lemon Yellow	13655	All but DN, PE, DF, JK
Finnish	DN-väri / Light Blue-Grey	35414	BL, LY, FK, DC, DB, DF, SB,PE, DN, JK
Finnish	Valkoinen / White	27778	BL, LY, FK, DC, DB, DF, SB,PE, DN, JK
Finnish	Sininen / Blue	25123	BL, LY, FK, DC, DB, DF, SB,PE, DN, JK
Finnish	Punainen / Red	21302	BL, LY, FK, DC, DB, DF, SB,PE, DN, JK
Dutch	Camouflage Bruin / Dark Brown	20045	FK
British	RAF Dark Green	34079	BL, LY
British	RAF Dark Earth	30118	BL, LY
Swedish	Ljust blågrå / Light Bluegrey	26176	DC
German	Schwartzgrün 70 / Black Green	34050	DN, JK
German	Dunkelgrün 71 / Dark Green	34079	DN, JK
German	Hellblau 65 / Light Blue Grey	35414	DN, JK

BL – Blenheim, LY – Lysander, FK – Fokker, DC – Douglas, DN – Dornier, JK – Junkers. DB & DF – Ilyushin, SB – Tupolev, PE – Petlyakov.

Warpaint

During the Winter War and the following busy training season, a great number of aircraft were damaged and sent to the factory for repairs. The various foreign aircraft were painted with local colours with the closest match. The totally differently coloured FIAT and Morane fighters were painted with the same tones in the Schildt & Halbberg Dicco colour range. This produced even more varying hues on the aircraft surfaces.

During summer 1940 new camouflages were tested in both theory and practice, by drawings and by painting real aircraft. In addition to the standard green, a dark grey and black were tried.

A partial solution was arrived at on 26 August 1940. The air force headquarters gave a directive: *All new warplanes are ordered, when painted during a repair, to be painted according to those instructions issued earlier concerning the painting of warplanes, irrespective of the present colouring of the aircraft.*

This meant in practice that warplanes (fighters, bombers and reconnaissance aircraft) were to be painted according to the *Tuisku* model, topsides standard green and undersides aluminium dope.

Only a month elapsed before new orders were issued on 30 September 1940, amending the previous stipulations:

Referring to 26.8.40, the following is ordered concerning the painting of front-line aircraft taking into account the tactical and homogenizing aspects:

1) *All warplanes are to be painted in a repair devoid of their present colours by the following instructions:*

  a) *Top and sides:*
    Kenttävihreä (Field Green) general colour (e.g. Winter 509), which is covered partly by dark grey pattern (darkness and shade same as the lower colour of British Blenheims) to break the overall effect.

  b) *Bottom:*
    Hopenharmaa (Silver Grey) general colour (as on Tuisku and in this case aluminium dope). Also fixed landing gear with this colour.

  c) *In winter conditions the tactical painting in point a) can be improved by an easily washable glue colour. Referring to last winter's experiences.*

  d) *Matt colours are to be used.*

2) *If there are larger amounts of aircraft paints in stock, they can be finished to replace colours in point 1) providing that they as such or by mixing are close in darkness and hue and tactically painted, particularly Blenheim bombers, are to be painted matching the original colours.*

3) *All earlier directives concerning the painting of warplanes are cancelled, except the 23.7.40 order for the national insignia and earlier for the serial numbers.*

Bristol Blenheim II serial BL-162 of 3/LeLv 42 ready for a mission at Värtsilä on 26 October 1943. (SA-kuva)

Tupolev SB serial SB-14 of 2/LeLv 6 parked at Helsinki Malmi on 20 May 1943. (Finnish Air Force)

The dark grey mentioned above meant the black underside of the Blenheim in British colours. The silver grey meant aluminium dope, but for mainly wooden and/or fabric covered warplanes it was Light Grey.

On 1 November 1940 the previous directive received an addition:

Concerning the previous, one Brewster was experimentally painted at the factory with given instructions. The air force headquarters points out the following:

1. *The Musta (black is used instead of dark grey) areas of the camouflage are to be enlarged so that the proportion of the black and green pattern is about 2:3.*
2. *The colour demarcation of the top and bottom surfaces is to be made wavy instead of a straight line, according to the attached sketch.*

    Taking this into account all warplanes are to be camouflaged thus, in the order told in the attachment sheet.

The first aircraft to receive the new paintwork was Brewster BW-379.

On 9 November 1940 the factory was reminded that FR-, PY- and BL- aircraft ordered earlier are to be painted according to the instructions given above.

Thus a standard camouflage pattern for the Finnish Air Force came into existence. It was named *SOTAMAALAUS*, which simply translates into "Warpaint". The aircraft were painted in this scheme at the factory during a repair or major overhaul. The field air depots servicing the front-line aircraft could paint the whole plane when necessary.

DN-Colour

The aluminium dope underside was considered too exposing in some front-line units. The comparison became possible, when German Dornier Do 17 Z (type prefix DN) bombers arrived in Finland in January-February 1942. These aircraft had RLM colour *Hellblau* RLM 65 undersides.

The air depot investigated the matter and wrote to the air force headquarters on 14 March 1942:

Based on tactical viewpoints we suggest that the undersides of the wings and fuselage of all warplanes should be painted light blue (matt colour) insteads of the present gloss Harmaa (Hopeanharmaa) (Grey and Silver Grey) paint. The arguments are:

Junkers Ju 88 A-4 serial JK-268 of 3/PLeLv 44 returning from a mission on 14 June 1944. (SA-kuva)

1. *Present gloss colour gleams in the sun when the aircraft bank.*
2. *Light blue matt colour better*

   Especially important to fighters. In negotiations with squadron personnel the same result.

The first application was done on 19 March 1942 to Blenheim BL-129, which was used in specialized high-altitude photo cartography missions far behind the enemy lines. The operating altitude was often 7,000 metres.

The air force headquarters informed on 7 May 1942:

Confirming the light blue matt colour, "DN-väri", *when painting the undersides of the wings and fuselage of all warplanes.*

Issued simultaneously was the splinter pattern for the upper surfaces of captured Soviet aircraft. The Warpaint colours were to be used. Painting was done at the factory or field air depots. Other minor paint jobs were done at the unit level. The paints for metal surfaces were manufactured by Warnecke & Böhm in Berlin, Germany and the wood or fabric surface paints locally by Winter Oy.

Amendments

In summer 1943 the aircraft factory shifted to a more angular pattern of the Warpaint.

On 27 July 1944 the factory received instructions to avoid the unnecessary painting of the whole aircraft. This was observed on a few Bf 109 G fighter, which received only the black stripes on the otherwise grey surface.

Warpaint existed until 29 September 1947, when the black paint was removed during the next repair.

Eastern Front Markings

In the middle of May 1941 Germany informed the Finnish military leaders of a forthcoming attack on the Soviet Union, due within a month. As a result mobilization took place in Finland commencing 17 June 1941.

As comrades in arms with Germany, the *Luftwaffe*'s yellow Eastern Front markings were applied to Finnish aircraft too. On 16 June 1941 the Finnish Air Force headquarters introduced these markings and two days later informed all flying and anti-aircraft units of new friendly markings on Finnish aircraft. They were a yellow 50 cm wide band around the rear fuselage, and the wing tip underside at a distance of 1/6th of the span.

The colour to be applied was Dicco 6 by trade name, a Rich Yellow colour used by the aircraft factory in small amounts for aircraft fuel piping. This was the same colour as German RLM 04, or British or American Insignia Yellow.

As 150 fighters were to be painted in a couple of days, and most of them at the units,

Blenheim I serial BL-120 of LLv 46 at Immola in August 1938. (Finnish Air Force)

Dornier Do 17 Z-3 serial DN-54 of 3/LLv 46 seen at Linnunlahti in February 1942. (Kari Stenman coll.)

Ilyushin DB-3M serial DB-13 of 3/PLeLv 46 taking off from Kemi in October 1944. (Kari Stenman coll.)

Blenheim I serial BL-111 of 3/LeLv 44 on a visit to Tiiksjärvi in October 1942. (Kari Stenman coll.)

neither the air depots nor the paint manufacturer possessed such amounts of the specified colour. A replacement was Unica 12 by name, a brighter yellow or lemon yellow colour, the application of which remains unknown. Simply because you cannot tell from the black and white photos, which one was used. In this book most of the colour profile subjects had only a single yellow and the regulation rich yellow was chosen for clarity.

The aircraft using only Dicco 6 were the Brewsters, since the planes were still without camouflage. On 19 June 1941 a State Aircraft Factory paint shop detachment went to the Brewster base and painted both the camouflage and the yellow markings on the aircraft, using the specified paints.

On 28 August 1941 additional friendly yellow markings were to be applied around the noses of single-engine fighters, at a width of 50 cm. Radial-engined aircraft conformed to this but in-line-engined ones had the band usually at 75 cm length. All fighters were to be marked thus by 1 September 1941. Depending on availability the colour could be either of the yellows.

In late 1943 the Air Depot investigated how to make the aircraft less conspicuous in the air by subduing the national insignia and yellow markings. Concerning the latter, no need was seen for alterations.

Below: Petlyakov Pe-2 serial PE-213 of 1/LeLv 48 at Onttola in August 1942. (Kari Stenman coll.)

When the Soviet main offensive commenced on 9 June 1944, just four days later orders were issued for instant removal of the yellow paint on the upper part of the nose. This process was done by 21 June 1944, out in the units or in the air depots or factory.

The Continuation War ended in a truce on 4 September 1944 and all remaining yellow Eastern Front markings were to be deleted within ten days.

Above: Ilyushin BD-3F (Il-4) at the air depot at Tampere, handed over to 2/LeLv 48 on 5 June 1943. (Finnish Air Force)

Left: Blenheim IV serialled BL-202 of 2/PLeLv 48 during spring thaw at Immola in April 1944. (Kaarlo Juurikas)

The decree for the Mannerheim Cross was issued on 16 December 1940, stating:

"Regardless of rank, a soldier of the Finnish defence forces can be nominated as a knight of the Mannerheim Cross in 1st or 2nd class, when showing exceptional gallantry, achieving important results in combat or leading operations with distinction."

This also included a grant of 50,000 Finnish marks, equal to the annual salary of an active *luutnantti*. A total of 191 solders received the Mannerheim Cross 2nd class in 1941–45, some posthumously and only four soldiers received it twice. The Finnish Air Force produced 19 recipients, seven of them from the bomber command, either pilots or observers (navigators).

The 1st class award was issued only twice, to *marsalkka* Carl Gustaf Emil Mannerheim himself and his chief of staff *kenraali* Erik Heinrichs.

SALMINEN Viljo Fritjof *lentomestari*

5.11.1941 Mannerheim Cross No. 33 as pilot of 1/*Lentolaivue* 44

"Brave and exceptionally skilful bomber pilot. During the Winter War carried out 49 missions and during the present war has flown 56 missions making a total of 105 missions. These include many far behind the lines covering both bombardment and reconnaissance. The last mentioned results were in most cases key to the successful land operations. E.g. on 4.7.41 he scored full hits on a moving train in a railyard and additionally blew up the fuel storages. On 7.8.41 he carried out a long-distance reconnaissance mission in spite of continuous harassment by enemy fighters."

Salminen Viljo Fritjof

KAHLA Paavo Elias *kapteeni*

26.4.1942 Mannerheim Cross No. 54 as observer of 3/*Lentolaivue* 14

"Vänrikki Kahla has flown 141 missions as an observer, showing phenomenal courage and judgement. In spite of obsolete aircraft and often-unfavourable weather conditions, he has carried out his missions in a commendable way. Reconnaissance reports by him have been reliable and very valuable to the military leaders..... On numerous missions vänrikki Kahla has faced enemy fighters, but with the help of his huge bravery, accuracy and judgement he has always been able to mislead the enemy fighters..... Luutnantti Kahla has since 24.12.1941 flown 16 sorties and participated successfully in the bombardment of enemy columns, camps and supply transports making several direct hits during the Karhumäki operation. Luutnantti Kahla has carried out all missions given to him showing extreme courage and judgement in spite of heavy enemy anti-aircraft fire."

Kahla Paavo Elias

WINQVIST Rolf Robert *luutnantti*

26.4.1942 Mannerheim Cross No. 55 as observer of 2/*Lentolaivue* 44

"Vänrikki Winqvist has participated in 75 missions as a bomber observer and shown in his work exemplary courage, fighting spirit, enthusiasm and skill. Out of the missions of vänrikki Winqvist 31 have been actual bombing missions and on 22 he has received direct hits in the target..... Luutnantti Winqvist has since 24.12.1941, after having recovered from the injuries caused by the 3.11.1941 crash landing, carried out six bombing missions, four of those to the Murmansk railway with excellent results in spite of difficult circumstances."

Winqvist Rolf Robert

Ek Rolf Birger

EK Rolf Birger *majuri*

8.2.1943 Mannerheim Cross No. 106 as leader of 2/LeLv 6

"*Both in the Winter War and the present war* kapteeni *Ek has acted highly successfully leading a bomber flight. He has personally participated in numerous missions, where he has shown exemplary judgement, skill and courage, thus being an obligatory example to his men. The enemy casualties caused by his bombardments are recognisable and of great value to our own warfare. Up to this point he has personally participated in the sinking of four submarines. Kapteeni Ek has flown 171 missions by 27.9.1942..... Kapteeni Ek has a high sense of duty and is a good instructor. His attitude to his superiors and men is military and pertinent. His example, enthusiasm and expertise have created the correct aggressiveness, willingness to duty and absolute performance to his men. Kapteeni Ek's flight has up to this point sunk eight enemy submarines and seriously damaged another two. The value of these accomplishments is even higher as the equipment used by the flight is obsolete and unreliable war booty.*"

Oksala Unto Johannes

OKSALA Unto Johannes *lentomestari*

21.11.1943 Mannerheim Cross No. 122 as pilot of 3/LeLv 44

"*Lentomestari Oksala has proven to be a brave, skilful and deliberate bomber pilot. Up to this point he has flown 102 bombardment and reconnaissance missions, most of which have extended far into the enemy rear and many of them at night, when special skills and endurance are required from a long-distance pilot. Lentomestari Oksala has distinguished himself not only in this war, but also in the Winter War, when he was rewarded with a gold watch as the most skilful NCO bomber pilot..... Lentomestari Oksala has performed all duties with exemplary courage and has shown in his action firm determination to win all difficulties and obstacles. The value of the actions of lentomestari Oksala is increased the fact that he has always most willingly volunteered for the most dangerous long-range missions, which are considered among all aircrews as the most dangerous form of missions due to the extremely great enemy fighter threat, which is the reason for the reluctance of fighter pilots to posted to long-range aircraft.*"

Iisalo Tauno Veikko Ilmari

IISALO Tauno Veikko Ilmari *kapteeni*

21.12.1944 Mannerheim Cross No. 168 as leader of 2/PLeLv 44

"*Kapteeni Iisalo has acted in a bomber squadron as a deputy flight leader and flight leader from the beginning of this war and carried out 124 successful long-range reconnaissance, photographing and bombing missions. During the advance kapteeni Iisalo has acted as a successful bomber of enemy transports, supply centres and air bases, and as a skilful and reliable photographer and scout. In spite of poor weather conditions, enemy anti-aircraft defences or fighters he has always most commendably performed his duties showing personal courage and skill..... Kapteeni Iisalo possesses a healthy amount of Finnish stubbornness, which has developed into strength of will and determination to carry out all missions to the last detail ignoring all obstacles and which has helped him to pull through the most difficult situations. By his personal example and energy he has developed his flight into a combat unit, which embodies the same unyielding aggressiveness and fighting spirit as himself.*"

Äijö Lauri Alfred

ÄIJÖ Lauri Alfred *luutnantti*

21.12.1944 Mannerheim Cross No. 182 as observer of 1/PLeLv 44

"*Luutnantti Äijö has acted as a bomber observer from the beginning of the present war and he has carried out 104 extremely successful long-range reconnaissance, photographing and bombing missions. The flights have to a great extent been directed far into the enemy rear and have thus required very much cold-bloodiness, judgement and in many cases resourcefulness. In bombing the enemy airfields, supply centres, and rear communications luutnantti Äijö has shown exemplary courage and skill. As a long-range scout luutnantti Äijö is extremely reliable and capable of judgement..... The losses caused by luutnantti Äijö to the enemy are certainly considerable and must have disturbed the warfare of the enemy in many ways. The reconnaissance results brought by him to the war leaders have been of greatest value. Luutnantti Äijö has made irreplaceable services to his arm and the defence forces.*"

Time	Number of airplanes	Squadrons	Target	Observations	Escort
05 Apr 1942 04.42–05.25	21 (19) bombers	LLv 42: 8 BL, LLv 46: 8 DN, LLv 44: 5 BL	Sekehe air base	Hits in shelters. Strong explosion. Several fires.	-
15 Apr 1942 04.58–05.07	19 bombers	LLv 42: 7 BL, LLv 46: 9 DN, LLv 44: 3 BL	Varbinitsi depots	Hits in target area. 3 fires. 3 BL destroyed.	-
31 Aug 42 04.00–04.35	22 bombers	LeLv 44: 8 BL, LeLv 46: 8 DN, LeLv 42: 3 BL, LeLv 48: 3 DB	Sekehe air base	Hits in target area. Several fires	-
20 Aug 1943 03.26–04.15	31 (30) bombers	LeLv 48: 3 DB+1 DF, LeLv 42: 5 BL, LeLv 46: 6 DN, LeLv 44: 16 JK	Lehto partisan training centre	Several hits in buildings.	12 MS
17 Sep 1943 21.25–24.00	30 (24) bombers	LeLv 48: 3 DB+1 DF, LeLv 42: 6 BL, LeLv 46: 6 DN, LeLv 44: 14 JK	Lavansaari air base	Haze, clouds and darkness prevented observations. 2 BL destroyed, 7 JK damaged	-
22 Mar 1944 15.19–15.22	25 bombers	PLeLv 44: 11 JK, PLeLv 42: 7 BL, PLeLv 48: 4 BL, PLeLv 46: 3 DN	Petsanoje motor sleigh base	Hits in houses and sleighs. High column of fire.	-
30 Mar 1944 19.42–19.53	31 bombers	PLeLv 44: 7 JK, PLeLv 42: 7 BL, PLeLv 48: 10 BL, PLeLv 46: 5 DN+1 DB+1 DF	Mergino air base	Hits on runway and shelters. Large fire	-
03 Apr 1944 20.29–20.31	35 (34) bombers	PLeLv 44: 9 JK, PLeLv 42: 10 BL, PLeLv 48: 10 BL, PLeLv 46: 4 DN+1 DB+1 DF	Kähy air base	Hits in target area. 23 fires. Explosions.	-
19 May 1944 00.02–00.07	42 (41) bombers	PLeLv 44: 8 JK, PLeLv 46: 6 DN+3 DF, PLeLv 42: 13 BL, PLeLv 48: 12 BL	Mergino air base	Hits in target area. Strong explosion. Several fires.	-
20 May 1944 23.30–00.05	43 (25) bombers	PLeLv 42: 13 BL, PLeLv 48: 12 BL, PLeLv 44: 8 JK, PLeLv 46: 7 DN+1 DB+2 DF	Alehovtsina depots	Rain prevented observations. 18 bombed reserve target.	-
12 Jun 1944 23.21–00.35	38 (34) bombers	PLeLv 42: 12 BL, PLeLv 48: 5 BL, PLeLv 44: 14 JK, PLeLv 46: 2 DB+2 DF+3 BL	Mainila-Kivennapa tanks, trucks and columns	Poor visibility prevented observations. 4 bomber reserve targets. 1 BL destroyed	-
16 Jun 1944 15.45–15.55	31 (30) bombers	PLeLv 46: 3 DN, PLeLv 48: 5 BL, PLeLv 42: 13 BL, PLeLv 44: 10 JK	Koivisto invasion fleet of 6 big and 30 smaller vessels	Hits among vessels. 2 big ships in fire. 4 full hits.	18 MT
19 Jun 1944 23.33–23.40	31 (23) bombers	PLeLv 46: 3 DN+3 DB+1 DF+3 BL, PLeLv 48: 5 BL, PLeLv 42: 8 BL, PLeLv 44: 8 JK	Humaljoen lahti invasion fleet	Hits among vessels 8 bombed reserve targets	-
22 Jun 1944 01.12–01.16	36 bombers	PLeLv 46: 2 DN+2 DB+1 DF, 5 BL, PLeLv 44: 8 JK, PLeLv 42: 13 BL, PLeLv 48: 5 BL	Häyry artillery groupings	Hits in target area. Strong explosion.	8 MT
30 Jun 1944 20.32–20.43	41 (40) bombers	PLeLv 46: 3 DN+2 DB+1 DF, PLeLv 48: 8 BL, PLeLv 42: 15 BL, PLeLv 44: 12 JK	Portinhoikka tanks and troops	Hits in target area. Few fires. 1 DN destroyed.	19 MT
01 Jul 1944 01.37–01.43	39 (37) bombers	PLeLv 48: 8 BL, PLeLv 44: 9 JK, PLeLv 42: 16 BL, PLeLv 46: 3 DN+2 DB+1 DF	Portinhoikka tanks and troops	Hits in target area. Strong explosion. 1 JK destroyed.	12 MT
03 Jul 1944 02.55–03.03	39 (38) bombers	PLeLv 44: 10 JK, PLeLv 46: 3 DN+2 DB+1 DF, PLeLv 42: 15 BL, PLeLv 48: 8 BL	Vakkila-Ihantala tanks, artillery and troops	Hits in target area. Strong explosion.	12 MT
04 Jul 1944 00.58–01.15	33 bombers	PLeLv 46: 1 DN+1 DB+1 DF, PLeLv 44: 7 JK, PLeLv 42: 15 BL, PLeLv 48: 8 BL	Viipurinlahti ship convoy	Hits inside artificial smoke screen. Strong explosion.	15 MT
05 Jul 1944 01.13–01.20	36 (34) bombers	PLeLv 44: 10 JK, 46: 3 DN+1 DB+1 DF, PLeLv 48: 8 BL, PLeLv 42: 13 BL	Tali artillery groupings	Hits in target area. Large fire.	9 MT
05 Jul 1944 20.16–20.22	34 bombers	PLeLv 44: 10 JK, PLeLv 48: 6 BL, PLeLv 42: 14 BL, PLeLv 46: 3 DN+1 DF	Äyräpää tanks and artillery	Hits in target area. Strong explosion. Several fires.	8 MT
08 Jul 1944 05.59–06.03	31 (30) bombers	PLeLv 44: 9 JK, PLeLv 46: 2 DN, PLeLv 48: 5 BL, PLeLv 42: 15 BL	Äyräpää bridgehead	Hits in target area. Several fires. 1 bombed reserve target.	11 MT
09 Jul 1944 12.00–12.01	33 bombers	PLeLv 44: 9 JK, PLeLv 46: 2 DN, 2 DB, PLeLv 42: 17 BL, PLeLv 48: 3 BL	Äyräpää crossing	Hits in target area. Huge explosions.	7 MT
10 Jul 1944 19.04–19.12	32 bombers	PLeLv 44: 9 JK, PLeLv 42: 15 BL, PLeLv 46: 2 DN+1 DB, PLeLv 48: 5 BL	Vuosalmi bridgehead	Hits in target area. 2 strong explosions.	12 MT

Date / Time	Strength	Squadrons	Target	Observations	Losses
13 Jul 1944 14.30–14.33	38 (37) bombers	PLeLv 42: 14 BL, PLeLv 46: 3 DN+1 DB, PLeLv 48: 10 BL, PLeLv 44: 10 JK	Portinhoikka artillery	Hits in target area. Strong explosion. Several fires.	16 MT
14 Jul 1944 02.01–02.05	35 (33) bombers	PLeLv 46: 3 DN, PLeLv 42: 14 BL, PLeLv 48: 10 BL, PLeLv 44: 8 JK	Käsnäselkä tank groupings	Hits in target area. Strong explosion. 3 tanks blew up.	5 BW 7 CU
14 Jul 1944 11.49–11.59	34 (33) bombers	PLeLv 48: 10 BL, PLeLv 46: 2 DN, PLeLv 42: 13 BL, PLeLv 44: 9 JK	Äyräpää tanks, artillery, troops	Hits in target area. Explosions. Large fire.	16 MT
14 Jul 1944 19.28–19.30	33 (32) bombers	PLeLv 44: 9 JK, PLeLv 46: 2 DN, PLeLv 48: 7 BL, PLeLv 42: 14 BL	Pitkäranta troops, trucks, artillery	Hits in target area. Strong explosion. 3 vehicles in fire.	5 BW 6 CU
15 Jul 1944 02.20–02.29	32 bombers	PLeLv 42: 6 BL, PLeLv 42: 16 BL, PLeLv 44: 8 JK, PLeLv 46: 2 DN	Äyräpää tanks, artillery, storages	Hits in target area. Strong explosion Several fires.	15 MT
15 Jul 1944 12.01–12.09	33 (26) bombers	PLeLv 46: 3 DN, PLeLv 48: 5 BL, PLeLv 44: 8 JK, PLeLv 42: 17 BL	Nietjärvi artillery positions	Hits in target area. 7 bombed reserve targets. Strong explosion. 1 BL destroyed	4 BW 6 CU
15 Jul 1944 17.30–17.32	27 bombers	PLeLv 44: 9 JK, PLeLv 42: 11 BL, PLeLv 46: 3 DN, PLeLv 48: 4 BL	Vuosalmi bridgehead	Hits in target area. 3 large fires.	13 MT
16 Jul 1944 12.37–12.40	28 (27) bombers	PLeLv 48: 5 BL, PLeLv 44: 7 JK, PLeLv 42: 13 BL, PLeLv 46: 3 DN	Vuosalmi bridgehead	Hits in target area.	16 MT
18 Jul 1944 06.02–06.08	30 (28) bombers	PLeLv 46: 3 DN, PLeLv 48: 5 BL, PLeLv 42: 14 BL, PLeLv 44: 8 JK	Vuosalmi bridgehead	Hits in target area. A few fires.	16 MT
22 Jul 1944 03.27–03.38	35 (34) bombers	PLeLv 48: 8 BL, PLeLv 42: 14 BL, PLeLv 46: 3 DN, PLeLv 44: 9 JK	Vegarusjärvi troop groupings	Hits in target area. Strong explosion.	5 MS
26 Jul 1944 20.27–20.29	34 bombers	PLeLv 46: 3 DN+1 DB, PLeLv 48: 7 BL, PLeLv 44: 9 JK, PLeLv 42: 14 BL	Kollaa-Näätäoja tanks, artillery, troops	Hits in target area.	6 CU 2 MT
09 Aug 1944 20.34–21.45	31 (30) bombers	44: 8 JK, 48: 6 BL, 46: 1 DN+2 DB+1 DF, PLeLv 42: 13 BL	Suojärvi station	Hits in target area. Warehouse blew up, a few fires.	6 MT

Right: Ilyushin DB-3M serial DB-16 of 2/LeLv 48 on the ice at Suomussalmi on 13 March 1943. (Kari Stenman coll.)

The table contains all regiment bombardments, where all squadrons attacked simultaneously the same target. The time informs the span of the bombing. The squadrons with strengths are in the order of attacks in each mission. The regiment strength informs the number of bombers taking off and in parenthesis, if mentioned, the number reaching the target. The observations are extracts of the mission reports.